SUPERCRAFT

EASY PROJECTS
FOR EVERY WEEKEND

SUPERCRAFT

EASY PROJECTS
FOR EVERY WEEKEND

DK

SOPHIE PESTER
CATHARINA BRUNS

CONTENTS

SPRING

SUMMER

AUTUMN

WINTER

DISCOVER YOUR SUPER CRAFT

A desire to work with our hands to produce something completely unique is one of the most fundamental human instincts. It is an urge that hasn't been lost in our consumerist society or in this digital age; if anything, it's growing stronger. These days, people make things themselves because they want to and not because they have to. Our office jobs, the stress of everyday life and the long hours we spend sitting at desks mean we do lots of brain work, but very little with our hands. And yet, creative handicrafts offer a kind of self-fulfilment which is all too often unattainable elsewhere in the modern world.

We understand the rewards to be gained from working with your hands, so we want this book to support your creative design aspirations. It offers 52 ideas for a whole year of Supercraft – from simple, but original and quickly accomplished little novelties, to more elaborate projects for skilled crafters. Whether you want to make something for the home or your wardrobe, for the garden or travelling, there's something here for you. Some of the creations can be made with children (the DIY lifestyle can't begin early enough), while others are for you alone, for when you want to treat yourself to a couple of hours of productive me-time, spent immersed in your hobby.

Do-it-yourself doesn't just mean knitting or crocheting; at its core it is far more important than that. It is about being independent, and, importantly, fulfils a desire to prove to yourself and other people: I can do this and it's fun! You hone your own skills as you develop from being a consumer to a producer and you become less dependent on easily available, ready-made offerings. Plus you have something covetable and truly unique to show for your work.

"Do more yourself" has become our personal motto. We are passionate DIYers, designers, and founders of Supercraft, which produces do-it-yourself kits for people who love being creative. Through the handmade market which we put on once a year, we know that these days there isn't just a demand to buy handmade products. Instead, ever-increasing numbers of people want to make their own lovely things rather than buy them ready made. We want to encourage this trend.

Making things with your hands is about having fun whilst being creative: expressing your individuality, maximizing your creative self-confidence, and realizing your personal visions. It's about making time for yourself and your passions. The most common excuse for not doing what you'd really like to is lack of time. But in reality, no-one has spare time – you just have to make the time for yourself. This book is a reminder to do that. It should say to you, "You can do this! Make something lovely."

Crafting has positively enriched and changed our lives and we want it to do the same for you. We have carved out jobs that we love around our passion for it. And it is much more than just making; it is taking things into your own hands and leading a creative, constructive life. Whether your dreams are big or small, doing it yourself is a way to make them come true.

The magic of DIY isn't in leafing through instructions or looking admiringly at projects. The magic comes in the doing and it begins the moment you get your hands working. So, let's get started. Discover your super craft!

We wish you lots of fun with your projects.

Sophie & Catharina

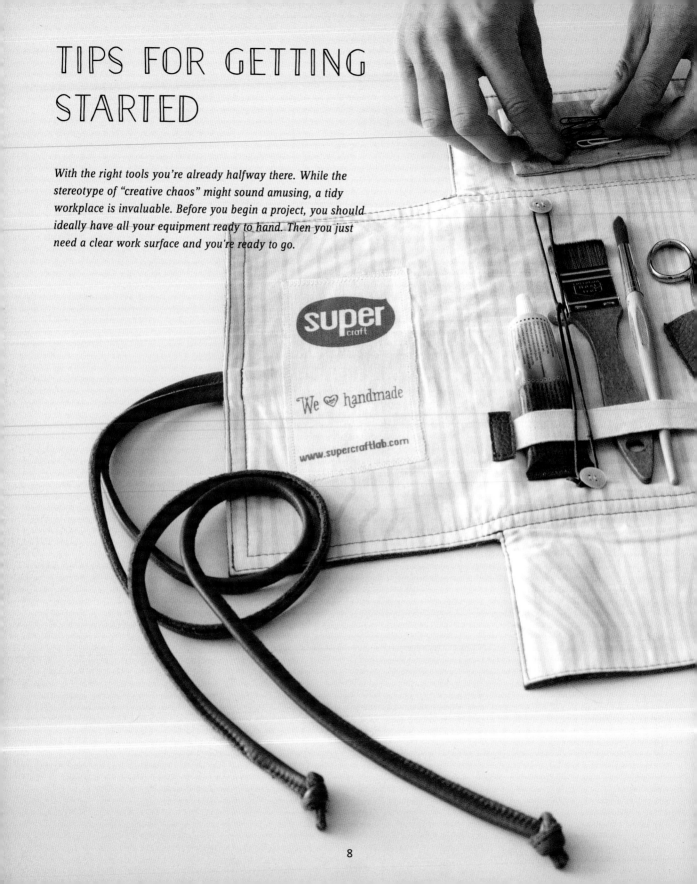

TIPS FOR GETTING STARTED

With the right tools you're already halfway there. While the stereotype of "creative chaos" might sound amusing, a tidy workplace is invaluable. Before you begin a project, you should ideally have all your equipment ready to hand. Then you just need a clear work surface and you're ready to go.

super craft

We ♥ handmade

www.supercraftlab.com

Basic equipment for making and constructing handicrafts:

- large cutting mat
- steel ruler
- scalpel or utility knife
- sharp scissors
- a couple of good paintbrushes
- acrylic paints in yellow, red, blue, white, & black
- little sponges
- various needles (sewing, embroidery, & darning)
- pins
- sewing machine and thread
- washi tape and double-sided sticky tape

- craft glue and fabric adhesive
- knitting needles and crochet hooks
- bulldog clips and paperclips
- pencils and felt-tip pens
- glue gun
- etching needle
- cigarette lighter
- iron and ironing board
- hollow punch and hammer

Have you got everything ready? Then it's full steam ahead – let's get crafting...

9

SPRING

"The wonderful thing about spring is that it always arrives just when you need it most."

German proverb

DANCING FLOWERS

Mobile making

Difficulty ★ ☆ ☆
Time needed 2–3 hours
You will need
7 rolls of baker's twine (1× mint, 3× pink, 3× orange)
20 plastic test tubes
mint green washi tape
scissors
small thin book, approx 10cm (4in) wide
steel ring 40cm (16in) in diameter

We love flowers! So we have come up with an idea for an easily renewable floral ornament that is both pretty and practical. This wonderful mobile is a simple but effective way to bring spring into your home. It's a lovely place to display freshly cut flowers, grasses, or plants, either from your favourite flower shop or that you've collected when out on a walk.

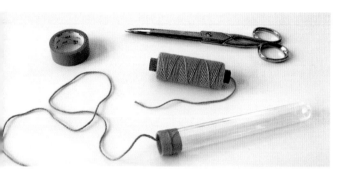

1. Cut a 50cm (20in) piece of the mint green twine. Tie one end securely around the mouth of one of the test tubes and neatly wrap washi tape around it to seal. Do the same for all 20 test tubes.

2. To make the tassels, wrap either pink or orange twine 35 times around the book and tie up all the strands firmly with an additional 20cm (8in) long piece of twine. (This will later be the thread for hanging the tassel.)

3. Slide the twine off the book. Tie all the strands together just below the knot by winding another piece of twine around it and tying it tightly. Cut through the loops. Make a total of 22 tassels, 11 each in orange and pink.

4. Hang the ring from four twine threads, as shown in the main image. Alternate tying one test tube and one tassel around the ring. Finally, pour a little water into the test tubes and place a single flower into each one.

Build a hanging garden

Difficulty   ★ ★ ★

Time needed 1 hour + drying time

You will need a thick branch, 2 small screw hooks, string, scissors, various Tillandsia plants, & a hot glue gun

Tillandsia are the ideal bathroom-friendly plants. Mounted onto a beautiful branch, they become an exotic little garden and an exciting home for your jewellery. Since Tillandsia take up water directly from the air, you won't need to water them if they're in a room where the humidity is high. Otherwise they should be sprayed regularly with soft water. The softness of the water is crucial, since lime clogs the plants' scales, causing them to die, even with regular watering.

Find yourself a lovely wooden branch next time you're out walking. Twist a screw hook into either end off the branch and hang it with string in a bright corner of your bathroom. Carefully stick on each Tillandsia with a blob of hot glue, being sure to let the glue cool for a short time first, so that the plants don't get burned.

JEWELLERY GARDEN

FAVOURITE MUG

Porcelain printing

Difficulty ★ ★ ★
Time needed 2 hours + drying time
You will need
white porcelain mug
personal photos or drawings
computer, colour printer
ceramic transfer film, compatible with your printer
scissors, iron

Do you have a favourite mug? The one which you like best for drinking your tea or coffee and which you're secretly grumpy about if someone else uses? No? Then you soon will! Since we are such great coffee lovers, we've naturally dreamt up something to personalize our coffee mugs. Become a porcelain designer with this simple project to make your very own customized mug, guaranteed to be one of a kind!

"Relax. Let go of the steering wheel. Meander through the world. It's a beautiful place."

Kurt Tucholsky

Take care when choosing your mug or other crockery piece that the surface curvature is not too great. Ideally you should attach the porcelain sticker to an area which only curves in one direction, or which is completely flat, as with plates.

The smaller the motif, the greater the surface curvature can be and vice versa. If the motif is too big there will be unsightly wrinkles at the edge of the sticker which will be difficult to flatten out. On the next two pages we will show you step by step how it's done.

1. Create your desired mug motif from your photos or drawings on the computer. Take care not to make it too big and to set out any writing back to front, as if in a mirror, when doing this. Then print the motif onto the transfer film. Let the print dry thoroughly.

2. Cut out your motif leaving a 1cm (⅜in) border. Cut an equal-sized piece from the transfer film. Lay the motif, with the printed side down, onto the shiny transfer film sheet and press down for four seconds on both sheets with a hot iron.

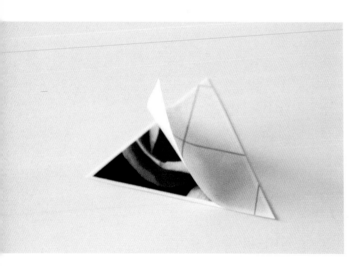

3. Let the bonded sheets cool, then cut out your motif with a 1mm (¹⁄₁₆in) border. Peel the transfer film carefully from the cut-down motif.

4. Lay the motif in a small bowl of lukewarm water. Wait briefly until the backing foil comes off.

5. Place the transfer onto your porcelain mug and carefully smooth out any water from underneath. Leave the foil to dry thoroughly for a couple of hours.

6. Preheat your oven to 150 °C (300 °F) and place the mug, complete with its motif, on the middle shelf for 25–30 minutes. Let the mug cool in the oven, then wash and use as normal.

Super tip

To enjoy your porcelain design for as long as possible, don't put it in the dishwasher. Wash it by hand instead, to preserve the colours and clarity of the print.

SEWN NOTEBOOKS

Paper embroidery

Difficulty   ★ ★ ☆
Time needed   2 hours
You will need
notebooks with strong cardboard covers
washi tape
etching needle
colourful embroidery thread
appropriate embroidery needle
scissors

With your own personalized notebook you'll never forget anything again! As two busy people, we know how important and practical notebooks are. You never know when inspiration might hit and you need to be prepared. This embroidery project is a really simple way to create your own, customized notebook. Cardboard is wonderfully suited to embroidery.

1. Make a copy of your chosen embroidery templates (pp.152–155). You can resize any of the letters during photocopying, reducing or increasing their size to fit your project. (You'll find details on this along with the templates.)

2. Stick the template onto the notebook cover with washi tape. Use the etching needle to make each stitch hole, keeping the other pages away and protecting the work surface with a piece of wood. Carefully remove the template and set about your cross stitching. Fix any loose threads on the reverse in place with washi tape.

"A little notebook and a great idea can change your whole life."

Working with leather

Difficulty ★ ★ ☆
Time needed 1–2 hours
You will need
1 piece each strong leather & soft calfskin,
each 30 × 30cm (12 × 12in)
utility knife, steel ruler
stitching awl, scissors, & cigarette lighter
spacing wheel for stitch holes 3–4mm (⅛in)
nylon thread with appropriate needle

Anyone who likes travelling knows that a handy wallet for your passport, tickets, a pen, and important documents is worth its weight in gold. We've designed a splendid leather pouch with room for the most important travel documents. Leather works well, but it's not everyone's cup of tea. For an animal-free version, try using felt instead. We no longer travel anywhere without one of these!

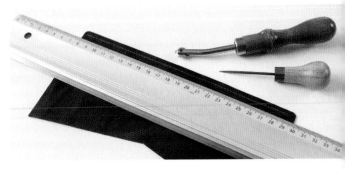

1. First cut the three leather pieces for the pouch to size, using the templates (pp.156–157); scale the template up by 125%. Cut the two incisions for a pen in the outer section, as marked on the template.

2. The dotted lines on the template show where the seams will be. On the two inner sections, use the ruler and the awl to draw carefully along the seams, then trace along this line with the spacing wheel.

3. Lay the inner onto the outer section as seen in the main picture. Now, protecting the work surface, punch firmly with the awl through every second point sketched by the wheel, so a little hole is made through both leather pieces.

4. Use the nylon thread to sew both inner pieces onto the outer section with back stitch (p.150). Pull any thread ends inside the pouch. You can fix them securely in place by heating them carefully with the lighter.

TRAVEL WALLET

BEADED BRACELETS

Make some arm candy

Difficulty ★ ★ ★
Time needed 5 minutes per bracelet
You will need
jewellery elastic
scissors
little glass beads
various jewellery pieces (bows, beads, & pendants)

Luckily friendship bracelets never go out of fashion - maybe because friendships are one of the loveliest relationships. Here we demonstrate a really simple version in which the beads are threaded onto a piece of elastic. Transparent jewellery elastic is perfect for making bracelets which slip onto your arm without the need for a fastener. A great project for kids and teenagers too!

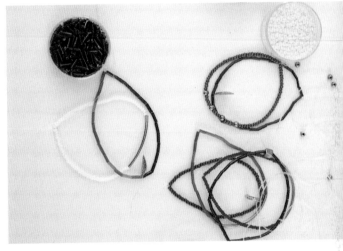

1. Cut a piece of the jewellery elastic 20cm (8in) long, or to fit around your wrist, plus some extra. Tie a double knot on one end so that the beads won't slide off. Now thread your beads, bows, or pendants onto the elastic in any pattern you wish, until the threaded beads fit all the way around your wrist.

2. To finish, tie the two ends of elastic together with a firm knot. Cut off the ends.

**"Everything is beautiful if it is contemplated with love.
The more you love the world, the more beautiful you will find it."**

Christian Morgenstern

Sew a cuddly toy

Difficulty ★ ★ ☆
Time needed 1–2 hours
You will need
felt 1mm (¹⁄₁₆in) thick, A4 sized, in white, light blue or pink,
grey or brown (2 shades), & black
scissors, needle, thread, sewing machine (optional),
toy stuffing, & white wool
hole punch, fabric glue
black embroidery thread, embroidery needle

Nearly every child has a favourite stuffed toy; a little friend who keeps them company throughout their childhood and so shouldn't be too delicate. Our sweet felt bunny has all the qualities needed to become such a companion, and it can be made in no time at all! All you need is a bit of felt, a needle, thread, and - if you want to be even faster - a sewing machine. This is a really personal present for your favourite little people.

1. Cut out all the felt pieces following the templates (p.158). Sew the white paw and ear pieces onto the body and ears respectively.

2. Now sew the fronts and backs of the ears together. Leave a space open at the end of each seam and pad out the ears with the toy stuffing.

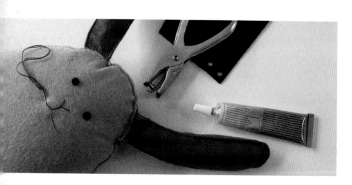

3. Stitch both body sections together in a similar manner, sewing in the ears as you go. Leave a small section of one seam open again. Fill the body with the toy stuffing, then sew the opening closed.

4. Finally, stamp out two round eyes from the black felt using the hole punch and stick them onto the bunny's face using fabric glue. Embroider a little nose and mouth using embroidery thread. Make a pompom out of white wool (p.155) and sew firmly onto the bunny's bottom.

FELT BUNNY

RAINBOW
CLOTHES HANGERS

Painting wooden clothes hangers

Difficulty ★ ☆ ☆
Time needed 1 hour + drying time
You will need
reclaimed, or new, wooden clothes hangers
rust converter (optional)
washi tape
acrylic paints in white, yellow, red, & blue
soft flat paintbrush

It's so easy to jazz up some plain wooden clothes hangers. These are quick to make and add a cool splash of colour to your wardrobe. The rainbow hangers really come into their own on an open rail, so they are also a lovely idea for boutiques and stores in which clothes or other items are hung out on display. Presentation is everything!

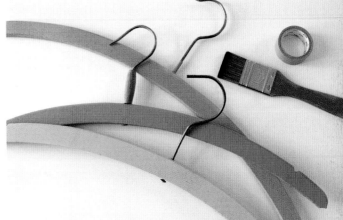

1. Old wooden clothes hangers, particularly if you've sourced them from a jumble sale, are often slightly rusted on the hook. Treat any rust patches with the rust converter. It's vital to follow the safety instructions carefully and to keep children away.

2. Tape up the base of the hook with washi tape so that no paint gets on to the metal. Using the acrylic paints in white, yellow, red, and blue means you can mix every colour of the rainbow. Apply the paint evenly over the wood with the paintbrush. Apply a second coat if needed. Allow the clothes hangers to dry overnight.

"Don't start with great intentions, but instead with a little deed."

German proverb

FLOWER CUSHION

Sew a circular cushion

Difficulty ★ ★ ☆
Time needed 1 hour per cushion
You will need
printed material & velvet, each 70 × 70cm (28 × 28 in)
scissors
sewing needle, sewing machine (optional),
with appropriate thread
300–400g stuffing per cushion
2 coverable buttons per cushion, 3cm (1¼in) in diameter

There's no question that piles of comfy cushions are a real enhancement to a cosy home. Our round flower versions are ideal as fine floor cushions, or just as good arranged on the sofa. This is a fabulous project for sewing fans who love unique living accessories - these cushions are so cool that everyone will want to have one. The material shown here, with the beautiful floral design, is available from our website (p.170). Of course, any other strong cotton fabric can be used.

1. Cut out matching circular pieces, 55cm (22in) in diameter, from the printed and velvet materials. Take care to ensure that any printed motif is in the centre.

2. Lay both fabric circles with right sides facing. Sew the layers together, leaving an opening of approximately 10cm (4in).

3. Turn the cushion right side out and sew around the edge, excluding the opening, using a 2mm (²⁄₁₆in) seam allowance. This makes a strong external seam. Stuff the cushion well with the stuffing and sew up the opening.

4. Finally, cover the two buttons with the appropriate material and sew them by hand into the middle of both sides of the cushion. When doing this, take the needle all the way through the cushion.

Book binding

Difficulty ★ ★ ☆
Time needed 1–2 hours
You will need
pages from an old book, scissors
sewing machine with thread
bulldog clips, etching needle
embroidery thread or crochet yarn, with appropriate
embroidery needle
sticky labels (optional)

Many memories often come in the form of little keepsakes that you'd like to have forever, but are unable to stick down in an album. This little book, made up of individual bound pockets, is perfect for the job. You can make one pocket for each day of a holiday and look back on them long after the trip. Or make one pocket for each month of a baby's first year. It's the perfect solution for keeping special mementoes safe and undamaged for years to come.

1. For each page of your journal you will need a large page from an atlas or old book. Fold each page in half and cut them all to the size you want.

2. Using a sewing machine, stitch together two of the open sides of a folded page, leaving one side open to create a pocket. Repeat this for as many pages as you need for the size of book you'd like.

3. Neatly stack the pages together and clamp them with the bulldog clips. Make sure all the open sides are at the top and the folded sides are on the right. Using the etching needle and protecting the work surface, make holes at regular intervals along the left-hand side.

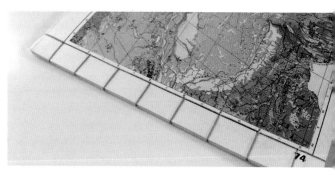

4. Pull the thread through the holes using a needle and Japanese-stle bookbinding stitch (p.151). Fill the pockets with your special items to keep them safe. You can affix sticky labels to the pockets, if you like.

TRAVEL DIARY

FLUTTERING
BUTTERFLIES

11

Folding origami butterflies

Difficulty   ★ ★ ☆
Time needed   1 hour per chain
You will need   assortment of square coloured paper, approx 10 × 10cm (4 × 4in), embroidery needle, small glass beads, sewing thread, & scissors

Lots of people know about the Japanese paper-folding craft of origami, but most consider it to be complicated. It doesn't have to be. There are also some simple origami projects which will turn out beautifully with just a little practice. These butterflies, for instance, are not difficult to fold, and when attached to a string they hang beautifully from any ceiling. Try them in any room that could be enhanced by a bit of movement and colour.

For one butterfly chain you need 10 origami butterflies. Pierce a tiny hole in the centre of each butterfly using an embroidery needle and thread them alternately with glass beads onto a long piece of thread. Knot a glass bead firmly in place beneath each butterfly; this way the butterflies don't all slip towards each other.

On the next two pages we will show you how to fold the origami butterflies. Put on some good music and let's get going. Have fun!

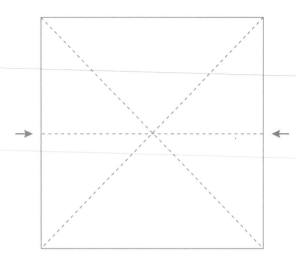

1. Fold the square paper along the dotted lines and open it up again.

2. Press in the horizontal fold (see arrows on Figure 1) to make a triangle.

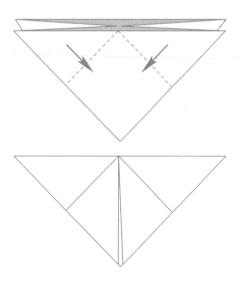

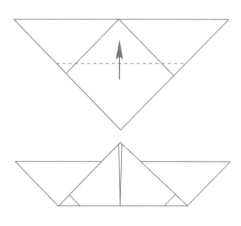

3. Lay the triangle in front of you with the tip pointing down and fold the upper left and right corners down towards the centre.

4. Now turn the paper over and fold up the tip so that it peeks slightly over the edge.

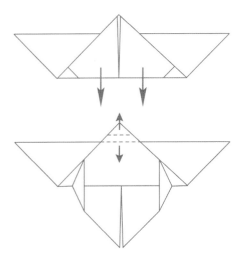

5. Next, fold down the two uppermost corners. This produces two little triangles on the left and the right, which you press flat.

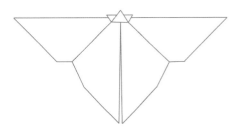

6. Now turn your almost finished butterfly onto the other side again and fold the protruding point back once completely and then halfway back up again.

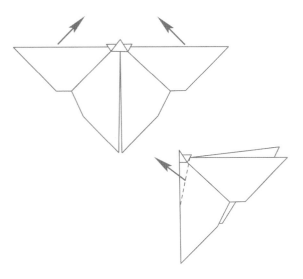

7. Fold the butterfly in half down the middle so that the two large paper surfaces are on the outside. Finally fold out both wings along the dotted edge shown above.

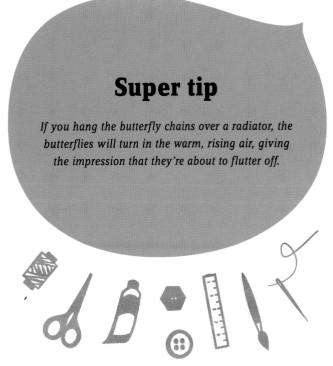

Super tip

If you hang the butterfly chains over a radiator, the butterflies will turn in the warm, rising air, giving the impression that they're about to flutter off.

Candle making

Difficulty ★ ★ ★

Time needed 30 minutes + drying/hardening time

You will need empty eggshells, candle wax (or old candle remnants), saucepan, egg carton, & wicks

Spring is a traditional time for lots of do-it-yourself projects. This is a classic springtime craft activity using eggshells, candle wicks, and wax to make special little candles which will enliven any table and would look great alongside a delicious Easter meal. Get the kids involved and make these. You could even use dyed eggshells, for extra effect.

Thoroughly clean the empty eggshells and let them dry. Heat the candle wax in a saucepan over a low heat until it melts. Put the eggs into an egg carton and carefully pour in the liquid wax. As soon as the wax begins to solidify, stick a piece of wick into the centre of the egg, so it reaches the bottom. Allow to completely harden, encouraging the wicks into the centre of the shells from time to time.

EASTER CANDLES

RUCKSACK

Sew a rucksack

Difficulty ★ ★ ★
Time needed 2–3 hours
You will need
quilted material, 120 × 50cm (48 × 20in)
soft, supple lining material, 120 × 50cm (48 × 20in)
scissors, pins, sewing machine, thread, iron, & needle
8 gold-coloured eyelets, 8mm (³/₈in) in diameter
2 small metal rings, 1.5cm (⁵/₈in) in diameter
cord to match, 6mm (¹/₄in) thick, 200cm (80in) long
fabric pen, nylon thread, & cigarette lighter
leather strap, approx 1.5cm (⁵/₈in) wide, 70cm (28in) long

You can never have too many lovely rucksacks. Whether it's for popping to the shops, stashing your sports kit, or simply as a practical bag for everyday use, the rucksack has proved itself to be an essential item. So why not make your very own? To make this version particularly classy we chose some quilted material, but any other strong fabric would also work as the outer layer. The pattern is casual and modern, a real eye-catcher, and works perfectly even with the most stylish outfits.

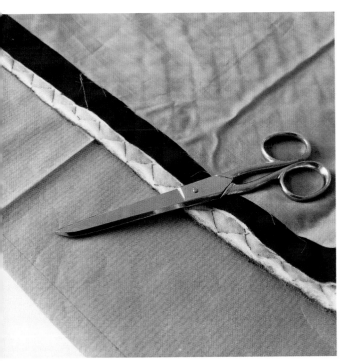

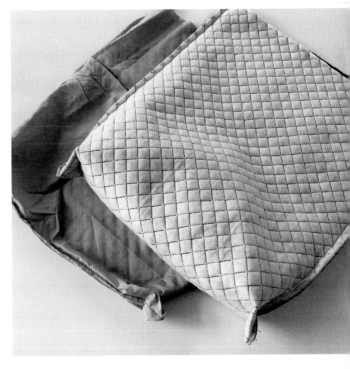

1. Cut out both pieces of fabric following the templates (p.159), taking care to follow the actual dimensions indicated. Fold the outer material in half, so that the right sides are facing, and pin along the edges. Repeat for the the lining material.

2. Sew up both edges on the outer material. On the lining material, leave a little part of one side open, as shown on the template. On both pieces, press the corners the opposite way, as shown above, and stitch across about 4cm (1⁵/₈in) in. This makes a strong seam.

3. Turn the outer material right side out and slip the lining material bag over it so that the right sides of both pieces are facing each other. Sew both bags together along the upper edge. When doing this, align the upper edges together, despite the 1cm (³⁄₈in) difference.

4. Now turn the rucksack through the opening in the lining material. The lining material will now be on the inside. Strengthen the edge of the rucksack with a second topstitched seam.

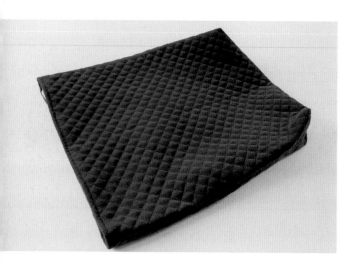

5. Finally, sew up the opening in the inner lining by hand. The basic body of your rucksack is now complete. Yay!

6. Mark the eight positions for the eyelets on the inner lining. Attach the eyelets to the fabric following the manufacturer's instructions. Take care to make the holes for the eyelets as small as possible, otherwise the material around the eyelets can easily fray.

7. On the outside of the rucksack, hand sew a small metal ring into the seams on both sides, as shown in the picture above. The distance from the base to the ring should be 10cm (4in). Thread the cord through the middle eyelets and then finally through the two metal rings on the sides.

8. Make a loop in the cord and wrap the ends firmly a few times with nylon thread to secure. Tie the ends of the thread tightly. Heat the ends carefully with the lighter to fix the knot.

9. Thread the leather strap through the two remaining eyelets to keep your rucksack closed.

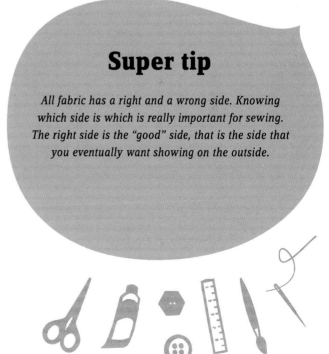

Super tip

All fabric has a right and a wrong side. Knowing which side is which is really important for sewing. The right side is the "good" side, that is the side that you eventually want showing on the outside.

SUMMER

"The real voyage of discovery consists not in seeking new landscapes, but in having new eyes."

Marcel Proust

CONCRETE LETTERS

Pouring concrete

Difficulty ★ ★ ☆
Time needed 1 hour + drying time
You will need
large, stong cardboard letters / moulds
utility knife
clear spray varnish
quick-setting mortar, depending on size approx
1 kg (2.2 lb) per letter
old bowl, spoon

DIY projects using concrete have been pretty popular for a while. Who would have thought it could be so simple to make cool, minimalist accessories from this traditional building material? We'll show you how to make your favourite letter of the alphabet using concrete and how stylish that can look as, say, a bookend. If you like, you can also brighten up your letter with acrylic paint. Suddenly concrete is not just useful for outdoors!

1. Remove the upper side of the cardboard mould with the utility knife so you have an open shape. Go outside in the open air and spray the inner surfaces of the mould carefully with several layers of the clear varnish, to act as a sealant. Allow it to dry thoroughly overnight.

2. In the old bowl, stir the mortar with a little water to make a thick, creamy mixture. Pour this into the letter. The concrete must be left to dry for at least 48 hours before being released from the mould, then left to dry for another couple of days.

Recycle a t-shirt

Difficulty ★ ★ ★

Time needed 5 minutes

You will need old, oversized cotton jersey t-shirt, scissors

No one knows for sure how it happens, but everyone suffers from the phenomenon of having too many baggy t-shirts in their wardrobe. We've got them, you've got them, and now they finally find a new purpose. Because these t-shirts can be transformed into fantastic cut-away shirts, whether for wearing over your bikini on the beach, or to pull on after a work-out at the gym; suddenly that old, far-too-big t-shirt will look really great again!

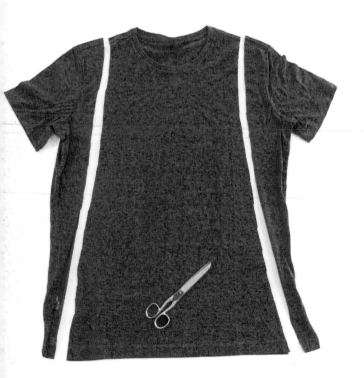

Lay your chosen t-shirt in front of you on the table and use sharp scissors to completely cut off the left and right sides from top to bottom. The cut edges of the jersey material will automatically roll inwards, so the edges don't have to be hemmed. Pull the shirt over your head and knot together the two corners on each side.

BEACH SHIRT

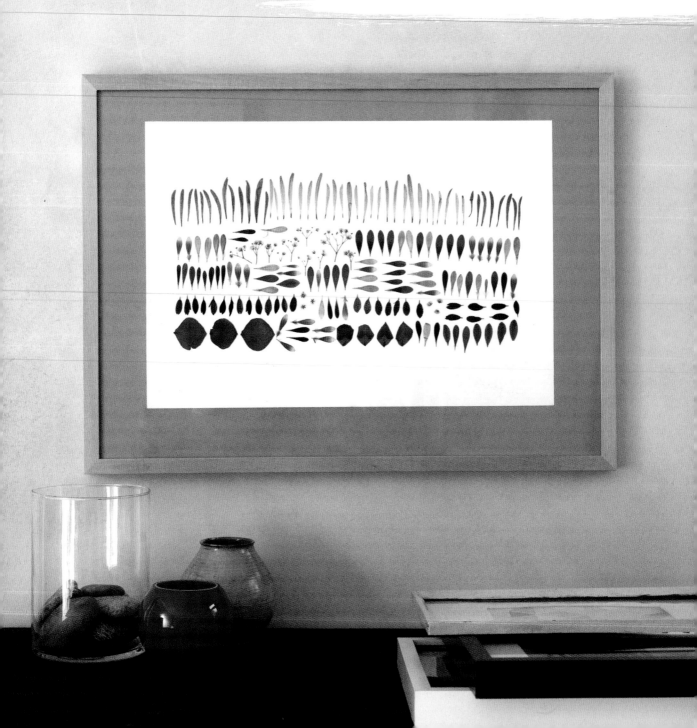

Pressing flowers

Difficulty ★ ★ ★
Time needed 2–3 hours + 1 week pressing
You will need
fresh flowers (eg roses, marigolds, & chrysanthemums)
newspaper, heavy books
thin paintbrush, water-soluble craft glue, & tweezers
watercolour paper, picture frame

You can make a true work of art using dried, pressed flower petals. A simple flower picture can be stunning enough to enhance any decor. The real pleasure is that flower petals can be collected almost anywhere, even if you're just walking through a city. Have fun discovering previously unnoticed flowers, leaves, and bushes, and preserve your summer with pretty framed petals. Now, get your eyes peeled and head out hunting!

1. To press the flower petals, pluck each petal or flower from its stalk and lay it between two sheets of newspaper inserted into open books. Close the books and pile them on top of each other, then pile even more books on top. Leave undisturbed in a dry place for about a week or so.

2. With the thin paintbrush, dab the glue onto the reverse side of the petals and leaves, holding them with the tweezers while you do so. Then, petal by petal, create your artwork by sticking them onto your watercolour paper base. Now frame your flower creation and hang it on the wall.

Fabric printing

Difficulty ★ ★ ★
Time needed 30 minutes + drying time
You will need star fruit, knife, kitchen paper, fabric paint, sponge, plain cotton scarf, & iron

No one ever tires of pretty scarves, and they have the ability to elevate any outfit – even more so if they are true one-off designs. A carambola, better known as a star fruit, is perfect for printing summer-style scarves, making the ideal, ready-made stamp. An alternative to traditional apple or potato printing, with a beautiful end result.

Cut the star fruit in half and place it, cut surfaces down, onto a piece of kitchen paper so that it dries out a little. Then, simply dab the fabric paint over the cut sides using a little sponge. Press the painted sides onto the scarf. For every new star you should dab fresh paint onto the cut sides of the star fruit. Distribute the printed stars evenly across the fabric, then leave to dry. Finally, fix the paint on the scarf by pressing with the iron, following the fabric paint manufacturer's instructions.

STARRY SCARF

HANDY KEY RING

Knot up a key ring

Difficulty ★ ☆ ☆
Time needed 15 minutes
You will need
nylon cord, 50cm (20in) long, 6mm (¼in) in diameter
multi-coloured nylon thread
scissors
cigarette lighter
carabiner hook

We don't know about you, but if we didn't have a key ring on every bunch of keys, we would spend our whole time key hunting. So key ring accessories are what's needed; ideally homemade ones! With a bit of cord and some colourful thread, this whole project can be completed in about 15 minutes. A key ring should be both pretty and practical; you almost always have it with you, after all. With our design, you'll never misplace your keys again.

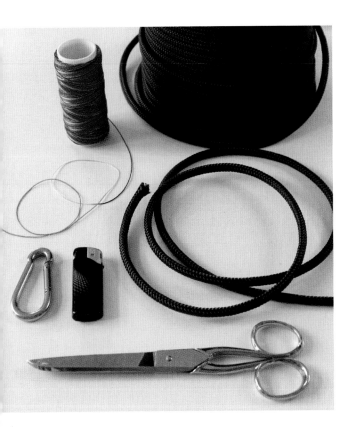

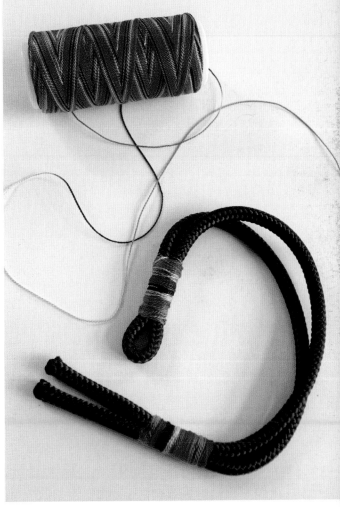

Fold the nylon cord in half and wrap nylon thread tightly around the loop end, then the loose cord ends, as shown in the picture (see right). Carefully knot the ends of the threads, melt them with the lighter and press down briefly. The cord ends can also be fixed by melting briefly. Clip the carabiner hook through the loop – and voilà!

SUNSHINE BEDDING

Printing with leaves

Difficulty ★ ☆ ☆
Time needed 3 hours + drying time
You will need
white duvet cover & pillowcase
newspaper, fabric paint
collection of leaves
sponge, sheets of felt
lino-roller, & iron

Nature provides the inspiration for another beautiful project. To make this unique, cheery bedding, all you need are some large leaves, fabric paint, and a desire to get creative! An eclectic mix of both large and small leaves looks fabulous. The bedding is washable, of course; just be sure to follow the manufacturer's instructions for setting, washing, and caring for the paint of your choice.

1. Spread the duvet cover or pillowcase out on a large table or the floor. Put a layer of newspaper between the two layers of fabric to make sure that the fabric paint doesn't seep through to the lower layer.

2. Lightly coat each leaf with the fabric paint, using the sponge, and lay it paint-side down onto the duvet cover. Place a felt sheet over each leaf and go over it with the roller a few times, pressing firmly, to transfer the paint.

3. Continue to print the whole duvet cover, spreading out the various leaves evenly over the area. For best design results, mix different sized and shaped leaves. Let the paint dry thoroughly.

4. Finally, fix the paint so that your new design will withstand washing. This is usually done with a hot iron, but follow the instructions given on the packaging of your specific fabric paint.

ESPADRILLES

Sew some shoes

Difficulty   ★ ★ ★

Time needed   3 hours

You will need

strong lining and outer fabrics, each 60 × 60cm (24 x 24in)

scissors, pins

sewing machine, iron

thread, needle, sturdy wool, & thin darning needle

pre-made espadrille soles in the appropriate size

In summer it's easy to dress in a fashion that's a little more laid-back than usual. Socks are a prison - feet need freedom! But going barefoot is not always an option, so a pair of custom-made espadrilles can save the day. This project is proof that homemade shoes can be stylish, chic, summery, and quick to make!

"Good times don't fall from heaven. We create them ourselves; they are hidden within our hearts."

Fyodor Dostoyevsky

1. Cut out all eight fabric sections following the templates (p.160). Lay the appropriate lining material on top of each piece of upper material, with right sides facing. Sew together these four sections to the relevant opening for turning, marked on the templates.

2. Cut the seam allowances diagonally at the corners and clip into the curves. Now turn each piece right-side out, shape the corners and edges neatly, and iron the fabric flat.

3. Sew up the openings by hand, ideally using blanket stitch (p.150).

4. Next, pin the fabric pieces in place on both soles, using the pins.

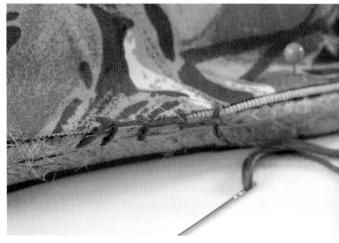

5. Thread the sturdy wool through the darning needle. Sew the fabric upper onto the sole.

6. Continue sewing around the entire sole of the shoes anti-clockwise.

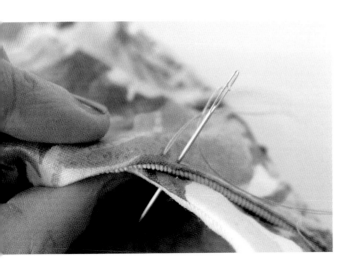

7 . Finally, use a simple backstitch (p.150) to attach both side pieces to the upper toe sections, to make the shoes more stable.

8 . Ideally, briefly try on the shoe before sewing together the two fabric sections, to test precisely where the final seam should be, so it will fit perfectly.

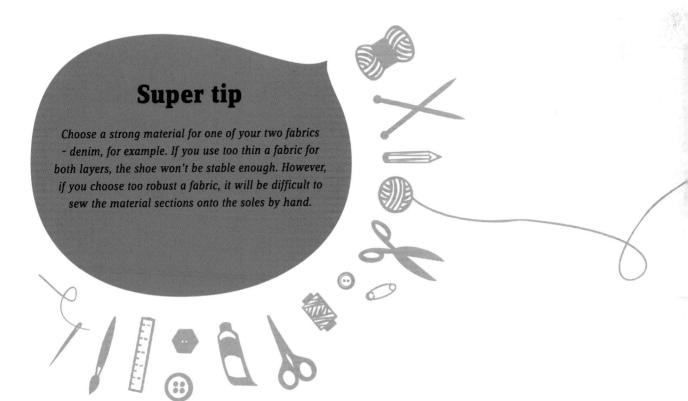

Super tip

Choose a strong material for one of your two fabrics - denim, for example. If you use too thin a fabric for both layers, the shoe won't be stable enough. However, if you choose too robust a fabric, it will be difficult to sew the material sections onto the soles by hand.

SUNNY LAMP

Spray paint a lampshade

Difficulty ★ ☆ ☆
Time needed 1 hour + drying time
You will need
pendant lamp with white (enamelled) lampshade
scissors
masking tape in 2 widths
matt spray paint in yellow
tweezers

This lovely warm yellow kitchen lamp will bring summer into every home. We made it using an original old lamp from a former factory. The industrial look is rarely out of fashion, so it should be easy to find similar lamps for sale. In a couple of simple steps, a cool, plain enamel shade can be transformed into a ceiling light that will turn any kitchen into a summery spot all year round.

1. Thoroughly clean and dry the lampshade. Cut the masking tape into small strips and stick them in a regular pattern on the lampshade. Take care to ensure the edges are pressed down onto the metal without any wrinkles, so no paint can get under the masking tape.

2. Outside, or in a well-ventilated area, spray a thin layer of the paint over the lampshade from a distance of 20–30cm (8–12in). Allow the paint to dry, then apply a second layer. Repeat to apply as many coats as needed. Once the paint has completely dried, carefully remove the masking tape using tweezers.

MANTRA GYM BAG

Printing with sunlight

Difficulty ★ ★ ☆
Time needed 2 hours
You will need
computer, inkjet printer
transparent film for inkjet printer
tape, newspaper, & a pane of glass
plain cotton gym bag
Lumi Inkodye in red and blue, large paintbrush

Summer, sun, light and colour. We recently discovered the photosensitive Lumi Inkodye, and ever since we have been beside ourselves with excitement! Printing using the power of sunlight? We had to try that out. And it really does work perfectly. Here we'll show you a kind of typeset textile printing, but high-contrast photos also print out well onto fabric. A true summer project which uses the sun as a tool.

1. Print out the motif (p.161) onto two sheets of film. Lay the two identical pieces of film on top of each other, making sure the design aligns perfectly, then fix them in place with some tape. By doing this the black surfaces form a greater contrast and keep out more sunlight.

2. In a dark corner, prepare the bag by laying it out on a stable, supporting surface. To keep the dye from seeping through, place newspaper between the layers of fabric. Then, brush red and blue Lumi dye onto the fabric using a large paintbrush.

3. Now place the film over the material which you have brushed with Lumi and lay the piece of glass on top. This way the film won't move in the wind while the dye is developing. Carry the bag out into the bright sun and wait for 30 minutes.

4. Once the colour has developed, carry the bag back into the shady house. Under the motif the material should be plain.

5. Remove the piece of glass, the motif film, and the newspaper. Immediately wash the fabric bag in the washing machine at 40 °C (104 °F) with a bit of liquid detergent.

6. After washing and drying, iron your finished bag and you're good to go.

You can use almost any object to create a design on your fabric, or paint the transparent film sheets by hand.

You can even expose pictures. To do this, print the negative onto two sheets of film and lay these on top of each other. The picture should be taken in black and white and it should be a high-contrast image.

Super tip

For the photosensitive Lumi Inkodye to develop its full colour strength, you need the UV rays from the sun. Since the sun is significantly stronger in summer than winter, this DIY project works best on a sunny summer day. It's worth waiting for the right day!

Dying fabric and trimming a tablecloth

Difficulty ★ ★ ☆
Time needed 2–3 hours + drying time
You will need
decorator's plastic dust sheet
white cotton fabric
white tablecloth
fabric spray paint in teal & pink
iron
scissors, fabric glue or sewing machine

Clouds and bunting flutter alongside one another here. This sweet tablecloth will be a hit at every children's birthday party. And, depending on the chosen design, it is also great for other festive occasions too. It will really come into its own at your next summer garden party! The trimmings waft beautifully in the breeze, meaning this tablecloth, with its cool colour gradations, will turn any old garden furniture into a fine table for a feast.

1. Spread the plastic dust sheet out over the floor. Soak the cotton fabric briefly in water and spread it out over the dust sheet. Spray the fabric paint onto the fabric.

2. Let the dye dry overnight. The next day, iron the material to fix the colour, then cut out long strips of semicircles and triangles from the material.

3. Using the fabric glue or sewing machine, attach these strips around the bottom edges of the table cloth.

4. If using glue, allow it to dry thoroughly, according to the manufacturer's instructions. Finally, give the glue an additional fix, using the iron.

FLUTTERING TABLECLOTH

HOLIDAY HAT

Trimming a straw hat

Difficulty ★ ★ ★

Time needed 1 hour

You will need straw hat with ribbon band; yellow, white, & blue embroidery thread or wool; embroidery needle, & scissors

When the sun beats down you had better wear some head protection, or you'll take a beating yourself. A hat is what's needed, but not any old hat - it should be a splendid hat! This embroidered holiday hat is a fantastic accessory if you find yourself at the pool, out on the balcony, or at the beach. To borrow from the words of Baz Luhrmann... If we could offer you only one tip for the future it would be this: wear sun protection!

1. The embroidery on the ribbon consists of an upright cross stitch and various satin stitches (pp.150–1). Stitch them all the way around the hat.

2. First, stitch the zig zag line in yellow. Second, stitch a white cross in each of the lower triangles and a blue stripe in each of the upper triangles. Sew up any thread ends on the inside of the hat.

"Enthusiasm is the most beautiful word in the world."

Christian Morgenstern

Bleaching denim

Difficulty ★ ☆ ☆
Time needed 1 hour
You will need household bleach, small glass bowl, denim shorts, old hand towel, & cotton buds

When we go through our wardrobes, we always find something that could benefit from a little make-over love. For example, an old pair of denim shorts. With a little creativity and the help of some household bleach, they can quickly be transformed into your new favourite item of clothing. Bleaching denim produces the most fantastic results. Regardless of the colour, length, or whether it's a jacket or a pair of trousers - denim always looks cool.

Pour the bleach into a small glass bowl, making a solution of 1 part bleach to 2 parts water. Lay the shorts on a flat surface and put the towel through the legs to separate the upper and lower layers of fabric. Dip a cotton bud into the bleach and dab it on the shorts. Repeat to build up the pattern, dot by dot. The bleaching can take up to 30 minutes to appear. Once all of your dots have turned white, put the shorts through a wash cycle.

POLKA DOT
SHORTS

MINI GIFT BOXES

Conjure up some confetti boxes

Difficulty ★ ☆ ☆

Time needed 10 minutes

You will need glue stick, colourful paper boxes, confetti or paper circles from a hole puncher

Creating impressive gift packaging can be incredibly time consuming. However, something quick can usually do the trick just as well - like this project. Both simple and functional, you can make these in no time and they look bright and cheery. Children in particular love these confetti boxes, but they will brighten anyone's day. Bring on the party!

Spread a generous layer of glue over the lid of a box. Sprinkle confetti or paper circles over it and press down well so that as much confetti as possible sticks. Let the glue dry, then shake off any loose pieces.

AUTUMN

"Have nothing in your house that you do not know to be useful, or believe to be beautiful."

William Morris

POMPOM
THROW

Embroider material and make pompoms

Difficulty ★ ★ ☆
Time needed 4 hours
You will need
material with a graphic print, or woven material,
of the desired size
embroidery thread in suitable colours, embroidery needle
coloured wool, large fork, & scissors

A nice heavy material is perfect for making a really simple throw blanket for your bed. We embellished ours with decorative embroidery and little woollen pompoms, to create a bohemian-style bedspread. This is great for adding a bit of extra warmth and colour to your bedroom, especially as the weather starts to turn a little chilly and the nights become longer. We've used a basic running stitch to embellish our fabric, but you can let your creativity run wild!

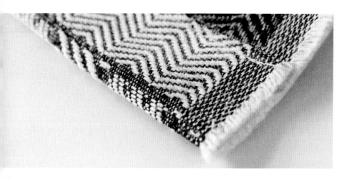

1. Trim the material to the desired size and hem the edges. You may be able to buy extra-wide fabric to cover your whole bed, or you might need to sew two pieces together to achieve the right width.

2. Use running stitch (p.150) to accentuate the graphic pattern of your fabric with the embroidery thread. At the beginning and end of each row, leave a bit of excess thread hanging over.

3. For the little pompoms, wrap the wool about 20 times around the fork, then tie it up tightly in the middle with a separate piece of wool, as shown. Pull the wool off the fork and cut through all the loops.

4. If you wish, you can give the pompoms a bit of a trim to make sure the strands are all the same length. Then sew them on to the ends of the embroidered lines, tie up the excess threads and cut them off.

Sew a scarf & make leather straps

Difficulty ★ ★ ☆
Time needed 1 hour
You will need
thin cotton fabric, approx 100cm (40in) square
sewing machine & appropriate thread
leather strap, approx 3cm (1¼in) wide x 90cm (36in) long
hollow punch, & 4 bronze D-rings, 3.5cm (1⅜in) across
4 bronze tubular rivets, 4–6mm (³⁄₁₆–¼in), & hammer

Using the traditional Japanese folding technique of "furoshiki" you can make a beautiful scarf and bag in one. Any scarf can easily be turned into a bag, then unfolded to be used as a scarf again. We've made ourselves a version with leather straps and use it for all kinds of different occasions, depending on the fabric and style. Anyone who wants to avoid using leather can use rope or cord for the straps instead.

1. Hem the square piece of fabric using the sewing machine. Do this by turning the cut edge over towards the inside twice by 6mm (¼in) so that it is tucked away and hidden inside the seam.

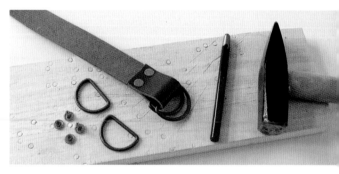

2. Next, make the leather straps. Fold one end over into a loop and use the hollow punch to mark two points where you want to place the rivets. Repeat on the other end of the strap.

3. Loop through two D rings onto each end of the strap (four in total). Fix each leather loop in place using two rivets, according to the manufacturer's instructions.

4. To turn your scarf into a bag, fold the scarf in half, then pull two matched corners through a pair of D rings and back over, down, and through the lower ring. Repeat with the other two corners and the opposite end of the strap.

FUROSHIKI
BAG

WALL-MOUNTED
ORGANIZERS

Make handy holders from felt

Difficulty ★★☆
Time needed 2 hours + drying time
You will need
utility knife, steel ruler, hollow punch, & 8mm (³⁄₈in) eyelets
2 sheets of 3mm (¹⁄₈in) felt, each 34 × 44cm (13³⁄₈ x 17⁵⁄₈in)
5 sheets of 1mm (¹⁄₁₆in) felt, each 20 × 30cm (8 x 12in)
fabric glue, embroidery thread, & embroidery needle
3 book-binding rings, 8, 4, and 3.5cm (3¹⁄₄, 1⁵⁄₈, and 1³⁄₈in)
in diameter

It's true that a bit of creative chaos in the workplace is a great thing - at least until you can't find what you need any more. To avoid that situation, you can sew yourself a splendid wall-mounted organizer out of felt. You'll have everything to hand, it doesn't take up any space on your desk, and it even looks pretty! The individual pockets can be varied and adapted according to your personal needs. A practical accessory which fits in even the smallest office, studio, or workroom.

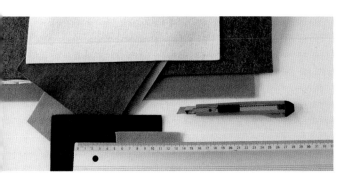

1. First, use the utility knife and steel ruler to cut out the felt pieces, either according to the templates (p.162) or to your own specifications. Make sure you scale them up, cutting the pieces out to the actual sizes indicated.

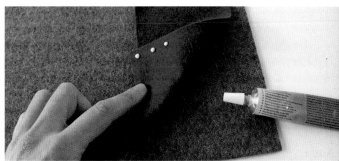

2. Stick the individual pockets onto both the large felt sheets using the fabric glue. Let the glue dry thoroughly.

3. Use the hollow punch to make stitching perforations in the felt, protecting the work surface with a piece of wood - the stitch length should be 1.5cm (⁵⁄₈in). Sew with embroidery thread, using backstitch (p.150).

4. Next, sew on the binding rings. Finally, secure an eyelet in the top left and right corners of the felt sheets, so that you can hang the organizers on the wall.

WOODEN
BLOCKS GAME

Graphic design painting

Difficulty ★ ★ ★
Time needed 1–2 hours + drying time
You will need
washi tape, stick-on dots
25 wooden cubes, 3cm (1¼in)
acrylic paints in red, yellow, blue, white, & black
small, flat paintbrush

This unbelievably simple wooden game is not just child's play to make, but it is also designed with children in mind. Kids can combine colours and shapes as they please to create their own patterns and designs. It's the perfect thing to take with you everywhere in a little cloth bag, to be pulled out when needed. A classic old-fashioned toy.

1. With the help of washi tape and adhesive dots it's easy to paint graphic designs on the wooden cubes. Just tape up the individual sides of the cubes, pressing the edges down well. Mix up the colours as you fancy. Use a few drops of water to thin out the paint and make the brush application smoother.

2. Use the brush to apply two or three thin layers of paint. Always let the paint dry thoroughly before removing the adhesive tape and beginning with the next colour, or another side of the cube.

SOFA CUSHIONS

Smocking fabric

Difficulty ★ ★ ★
Time needed 3 hours
You will need
black-and-white patterned fabric with stripes, checks, &
polka dots, each 100cm (40in) square
black embroidery thread, needle, pins, & scissors
fabric for the cushion backs, each 60cm (24in) square
zip 40cm (16in) long, & cushion pad 50cm (20in) square
sewing machine & appropriate thread

Cool sofa cushions don't always have to come from an expensive shop. If you want to give your sofa an individual touch, you're best off making your own cushions - smocked ones, in fact! This interesting technique involves folding the material and produces a really pretty final effect. We will show you three simple variants with impressive results. Comfort can be really stylish!

1. First smock the black-and-white patterned material. To do this, follow the very simple principles illustrated at the back of the book (p.163). The finished smocked area should measure roughly 45cm (18in) square.

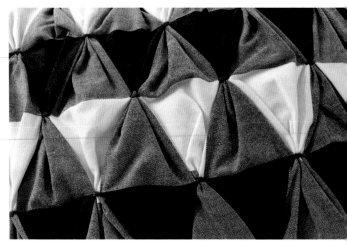

2 . Following the smocking technique, the polka dot fabric comes together to produce little flower shapes. .

3 . On checked fabric, the pattern is folded to create triangles when smocked.

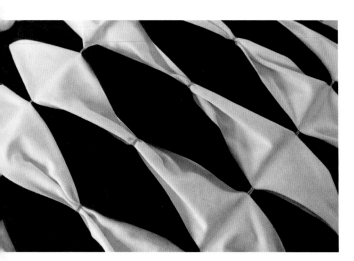

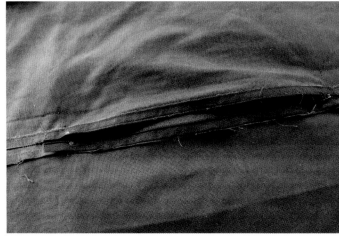

4 . From stripes, little diamonds are produced. When you have smocked an area measuring roughly 45cm (18in) square, secure any folds outside the smocked area using pins. For the cushion front you will need a piece of fabric approximately 50cm (20in) square. Cut off any excess.

5 . Cut the back fabric in half. Centre and pin the zip in place between the two pieces, then sew it in place to create the cushion back. Open the zip.

6 . Now lay the two halves of the cushion cover, right sides together, and pin around the edges. Sew up along all four sides. Cut off the excess seam allowance at the corners diagonally, as shown. This will reduce the bulk in the corners when you turn the cover right side out.

7 . Finally turn out the cushion cover right side out, through the open zip, and stuff with the cushion pad.

Super tip

Don't sew the cushion cover to be larger than your cushion pad, or your cushion will look flat. Better to make it 1cm (³/₈in) smaller than the cushion pad. It doesn't look good if the cushion covering is much too big and smocked cushion covers, in particular, need to be well stuffed.

CLOAKROOM
TIDY

Crochet a bag

Difficulty ★ ★ ☆

Time needed 1–2 hours

You will need

10 x 50g balls of thick soft white wool; we used Rowan Kidsilk Creation: 10m; 70% mohair, 30% silk

20mm crochet hook

stitch marker

yarn needle

It's the same for everyone isn't it? Particularly in winter, the cloakroom rapidly descends into an unmanageable assortment of jackets, scarves, gloves, and mittens. How great would it be if these items were always to hand and the cloakroom stayed nice and tidy? Well, it's possible! All your accessories will fit into this practical crocheted basket without everything ending in disarray. You can't crochet? You can now, with our basic techniques (p.146).

Work 6 chain stitches (sts); join to form a ring

Round 1: 12 dc into ring. (12 sts)

Round 2: 1dc in first st, 2dc in next st, *1dc in next st, 2dc in next st, rep from * to end. (18 sts)

Round 3: *1dc in first 2 sts, 2dc in next st, *1dc in next 2 sts, 2dc in next st; rep from * to end .(24 sts)

Round 4: *1dc in first 3 sts, 2dc in next st, *1dc in next 3 sts, 2dc in next st; rep from * to end. (30 sts)

Round 5: 1dc in each st.

Round 6: *1dc in first 4 sts, 2dc in next st, *1dc in next 4 sts, 2dc in next st; rep from * to end. (36 sts)

Round 7: *1dc in each st.

Round 8: *1 dc in first 5 sts, 2dc in next st, *1dc in next 5 sts, 2dc in next st; rep from * to end. (42 sts)

Rounds 9 to 15: 1dc in each st.

Round 16: 1dc in first 5 sts, dc 2 sts together, *1dc in next 5 sts, dc 2 sts together; rep from * to end. (36 sts)

Round 17: 1dc in each st.

Round 18: 1dc in first 4 sts, dc 2 sts together, *1dc in next 4 sts, dc 2 sts together; rep from * to end. (30 sts)

Round 19: 1dc in first 3 sts, dc 2 sts together, *1dc in next 3 sts, dc 2 sts together; rep from * to end. (24 sts)

Turn the crocheted sphere. In one point along the edge, crochet a short loop consisting of 14 chain stitches and work 2 rows of dc in each st.

Sew in all yarn ends.

PAGE HOLDER

Create a bookmark

Difficulty ★ ☆ ☆
Time needed 30 minutes
You will need small pieces of card (eg flyers, postcards), utility knife, steel ruler, cutting board, & washi tape

These slim little bookmarks are perfect if you need to keep your place in lots of different spots in various books; for example, when you're writing up a project, or revising for exams. The little flap offers room for all kinds of reminders, business cards, and notes, or it can be labelled as a reminder of why you bookmarked that page. Your favourite recipe in a cook book will always be easy to find. They're really handy, so be sure to make lots and lots of them.

1. For every bookmark you will need two equally sized pieces of card, each 13.5 × 6.5cm (5⅜ × 2⅝in). On one piece, cut off the upper left edge diagonally, beginning the cut at a height of 3.5cm (1⅜in) from the lower left corner and finishing it at the upper right corner.

2. Lay both the card pieces on top of each other and stick the lower and right edges together with washi tape. Fold the little corner of excess tape on the upper right side inwards, so that it is hidden.

"Work which we enjoy becomes a pleasure."

William Shakespeare

Three-stranded knitting

Difficulty ★ ★ ☆
Time needed 3 hours
You will need 3 x 50g balls of double-knit yarn; we used LAMANA Cusco: 100% Alpaca
7mm circular knitting needle 40cm (16in) long, stitch marker, yarn needle, scissors, & leather label (optional)

Knitting is more popular than ever. And why not? Nowadays knitting your own cool accessories, working with wool, and choosing from the vast array of inspiring patterns is often a first step into the world of making things yourself. This warm and cosy hat is knitted with three strands of yarn at the same time, so is ready very quickly once you have taught yourself the knitting basics from our course (p.140). Bring on winter!

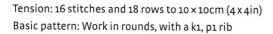

Tension: 16 stitches and 18 rows to 10 × 10cm (4 × 4in)
Basic pattern: Work in rounds, with a k1, p1 rib

Cast on 64 stitches, working with 3 strands at once. Join in the round. Work 20cm (8in) in k1, p1 rib.

Next row: Rep (k2tog, work 6 sts in rib) to end of round.
Next row: Rep (k2 tog, work 5 sts in rib) to end of round.
Next row: Rep (k2 tog, work 4 sts in rib) to end of round.
Next row: Rep (k2 tog, work 3 sts in rib) to end of round.
Next row: Rep (k2 tog, work 2 sts in rib) to end of round.
Next row: Rep (k2 tog, p1) to end of round. (16 sts)
There should be a continuous rib in a decreasing circle.

Since the number of stitches gradually decreases, the stitches will no longer fit around the circular needle without considerable stretching of the yarn. So that you don't have to play a constant game of changing needles, pull the circular needle cord out between the stitches at one location and push the stitches towards the needles until you have sufficient space to knit again.

Cut off the yarn, leaving a generous strand, and use a yarn needle to thread the yarn through the remaining 16 stitches. Sew up firmly. Dampen the hat briefly by placing it under a wet towel, then leave it to dry. Sew in any loose ends and sew on your label, if using.

SNUGGLY
BEANIE HAT

PLAITED RUG

Weave a runner

Difficulty ★ ★ ☆
Time needed 3–4 hours
You will need

t-shirt yarn in the colours of your choice (approx. 11m/37ft per plait; 220m/740ft total)

scissors, glue gun

5 pieces of felt, each 34 × 44cm (13⅝ × 17⅝in) for a rug of 45 × 170cm (18in × 5ft 8in), or pieces of felt to make up a rug of your desired size)

A rug is something you can make yourself, and quite easily too – with a bit of patience you can even make a pretty large one, depending on the space you have to fill. The example here is really lovely and definitely useful for everyday life as a narrow runner in the hall or as a mat in the bathroom or bedroom. At last you can have a rug in your favourite colours, perfect for a particular spot, woven yourself, and absolutely unique.

1. Cut three pieces of t-shirt yarn, each 370cm (12ft 4in) in length. Fold them in half and knot them together at the folded end. Attach the knot to a door handle. Make a plait using two strands together at a time.

2. For a 45cm- (18in-) wide rug, you need approximately 20 plaits, each 170cm (5ft 8in) long.

3. Use the glue gun to stick the individual plaits row by row onto the felt sheets, laying each one next to its neighbour. Keep doing this until the entire surface of felt is densely covered with the plaits.

4. If your plaits are somewhat longer than the felt sheet, just unravel them a little and re-knot them a bit further back. Finally, trim the fringed edges to the same length.

CUSTOMIZED
DISPLAY CABINET

Design a collector's cabinet

Difficulty ★ ☆ ☆
Time needed 1 hour
You will need collector's cabinet, coloured paper, utility knife, steel ruler, cutting board, & glue stick

Have you still got an old collector's cabinet at home? Originally, these cases were intended for organizing typesetting letters for printing, but nowadays they are mostly used as a really pretty and practical wall decoration. From children's milk teeth to little figurines or buttons, anything you consider to be precious will find a home here. We have jazzed up one of these old collector's cabinets using some very simple materials.

You may find one of these old wooden display units at a jumble sale, or have one at home crying out for an update. Use coloured paper or memorable photos to decorate the back of individual compartments, carefully cutting the paper to fit inside each box. When it's done, hang it on a wall and fill it with memories.

French knitting

Difficulty ★★☆

Time needed 4–5 hours

You will need

French knitting doll, 3.5cm (1⅜in) in diameter, with 8 hooks

2 x 50g balls of fine yarn; we used LAMANA Cusi in denim blue and silvery grey: 225m; 100% Alpaca

2–3mm crochet hook, yarn needle

pendant lamp, with fabric cable & porcelain fitting

Do you still remember the good old French knitting doll? The DIY tool we all used to create endless knitted tubes without really knowing what to do with them? Well, they are perfect for covering cords. Nowadays the old wooden French knitting dolls have been replaced by plastic varieties. The end result of this project is a knitted tube which will turn a minimalist lamp into a homely accessory. Go and grab your knitting doll, it's really good fun!

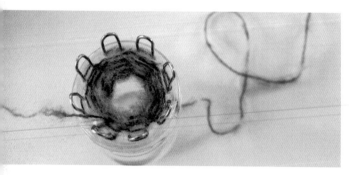

1. With the French knitting doll, knit a tube which is at least as long as the power cable for the lamp. Knit with both strands of yarn in parallel to maintain the mottled appearance of the knitted tube.

2. Cast off the completed tube from the knitting doll and slip it over the lamp cord.

3. Take care that the knitted tube does not touch the bulb or the exposed electrical wires! Finally, sew in any loose threads.

4. Important: Get an electrician to help you with the lamp installation. Don't try to connect the power cable yourself!

KNITTED
LAMP CORD

FAIRY LIGHTS

Fold origami lanterns

Difficulty ★ ★ ☆
Time needed   2 hours
You will need
origami paper with pretty patterns, each approx 20cm (8in)
square; 80 g/m² (gsm)
LED fairy lights

A little chain of fairy lights will make any room more homely – it's not just something for a child's bedroom. Folded origami lanterns along a simple chain of fairy lights conjures up a really special atmosphere. Thanks to the colours and patterns, they produce warm, indirect illumination. A splendid project, perfect year round.

1. Fold a square of origami paper diagonally twice, then fold the sheet of paper horizontally and vertically. Open the paper back out.

2. Press in the two opposite edges so that you get a triangle, as shown above. Press down with your thumb to crease all the edges well.

"Oh, what magic there is in this little word: home!"

Emmanuel Geibel

3. Turn so the triangle points away from you. Next, fold the two corners closest to you upwards, towards the centre, making two new smaller triangles.

4. Turn over the origami paper and fold the other two corners likewise towards the centre.

5. Now fold the two corners shown in the picture into the centre. Turn the paper over and repeat this step on the other side.

6. Now fold the tiny corners upwards, as depicted here.

7 . Now, take the folded-up corners and bend them halfway back again.

8 . You will have two little triangles which can now be pushed between the folds of the existing triangles beneath. Repeat from step 6 with the corners on the other side.

9 . The resulting paper shape has a little opening at one end. Blow carefully into this opening until the lantern has reached its full size.

10 . Attach the lanterns one by one to the little LED bulbs on your fairy chain. Only use LED lights: regular bulbs become hot and create a fire hazard.

WOOLLY PURSE

39

Decorate a canvas and sew a purse

Difficulty ★ ★ ☆

Time needed 4 hours

You will need

cross stitch canvas 20 × 30 cm (8 × 12in) in 8 count (35 holes per 10cm [4in])

embroidery wool in white, yellow, orange, 3 shades of green, & dark red

flex frame bag closure 12cm (4¾in) long), scissors

embroidery needle, cotton thread, & sewing machine

Embroidery is addictive and very easy to learn. This purse, with its simple cross stitch, is a lovely project to inculcate yourself with a passion for embroidery. Thanks to the design and the wool, the pouch is very strong and ideal for use as a purse or little bag when you're on the go. It is big enough to hold business cards and credit cards and, thanks to the snap fastening, coins and notes can also be safely stashed inside.

1. Hem both short edges of the canvas, creating channels 2cm (¾in) wide. These channels will later be used to hold the flex frame. The arrows in the image above show where they will be in relation to the finished embroidery design.

2. Embroider the motif centrally on the canvas, following the template (p.164), using a half cross stitch with a single thread. Sew in all the loose ends on the rear. Do not embroider the reverse side of the frame channels.

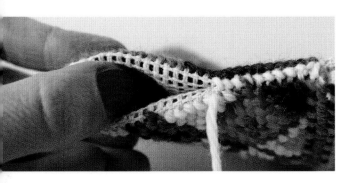

3. Trim the unstitched edges of the canvas to make a border of 2.5cm (1in) and hem it once with the sewing machine. Fold the purse in half and sew up the sides by hand using white embroidery wool.

4. Stitch up the edges of your channels likewise by hand to prevent the canvas from fraying, but do not sew them closed. Finally, insert the open flex frame into each of the channels before sewing them shut.

WINTER

"It is not what things really are, but rather what we perceive them to be which makes us happy or unhappy."

Arthur Schopenhauer

DOOR ORNAMENT

40

Paper flower folding

Difficulty ★ ☆ ☆
Time needed 2 hours
You will need
thin crafting crepe paper in red, pink, & pale yellow
scissors, craft glue
baker's twine in pink and red
pale yellow washi tape
straw wreath

Crepe paper is absolutely fantastic for making large paper flowers and, because they never wilt, they make a particularly fine door ornament. This Christmassy red wreath will spread the festive spirit, but it can be used throughout the year and adorned with new colours and flowers. It gives every visitor a warm welcome.

For the individual flowers you will need crepe paper in at least three different shades of red and pink, as well as a pale yellow for the stamens.

1 . For one flower, cut out four 50 × 12 cm (20 x 4¾in) pieces of crepe paper. Lay these one on top of the other and fold them concertina fashion into a narrow strip 3cm (1¼in) wide.

2 . Tie the centre of the paper strip firmly with a piece of matching baker's twine.

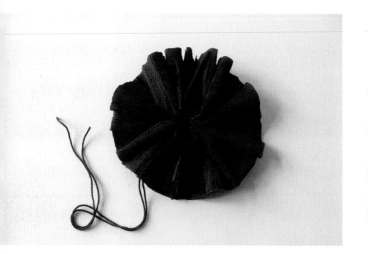

3 . Next, fan out the paper. Begin pulling each individual layer of paper up and towards the middle to form a half-sphere.

4 . When you've pulled all the paper layers into shape, the result is a flower.

5. Now you just need a lovely stamen for the centre of the flower. To make this, roll up a thin strip of yellow crepe paper and secure one end with washi tape. Cut into the non-secured end to create a fringe.

6. Tease out the individual fringes of the stamen from each other. Carefully push back the flower petals so you can see the centre and stick the stamen into the centre of the flower with a blob of craft glue.

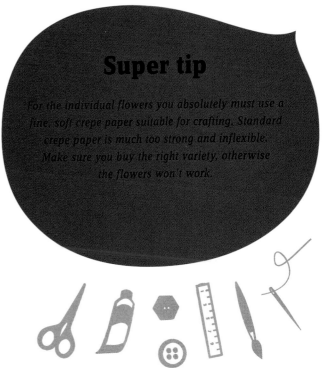

Super tip

For the individual flowers you absolutely must use a fine, soft crepe paper suitable for crafting. Standard crepe paper is much too strong and inflexible. Make sure you buy the right variety, otherwise the flowers won't work.

7. Tie the individual flowers around the straw wreath until it is full. You can cut off the ends of the baker's twine or leave them hanging.

Felt embroidery

Difficulty ★ ☆ ☆
Time needed 1 hour
You will need
felt tote bag
black felt pen
hollow punch, hammer
suitable needle for the wool, scissors
pale blue wool, or any other colour of your choice

"Reuse and recycle" are terms closely associated with DIY culture. And, indeed, why should we always take a new plastic bag for every purchase? More eco-friendly and attractive is your own handmade bag, which is not only really durable, but also strong enough to bring heavy shopping home safely. Felt is the ideal material for the job and it is great for embroidering.

1. Transfer dots for your embroidery from the template (p.165) onto the bag with the pen. Use the punch and hammer to stamp holes through the marks, placing a piece of wood underneath to protect your work surface.

2. Thread the needle with the wool and stitch the design, creating your own pattern if you prefer (see photo, right, for some inspiration). For stronger lines, use double strands of wool.

TOTE BAG

BESPOKE
STATIONERY

42

Make writing paper

Difficulty ★ ★ ★
Time needed 1 hour + drying time
You will need
watercolours, paintbrush
watercolour pad
utility knife, steel ruler, & glue stick
writing paper and envelopes, made from handmade paper
heavy books

A handwritten letter is surely one of the most personal things that anyone can receive. Despite this age of computers and the digital revolution, the desire for individual, completely personal things hasn't gone away. Having your own stationery for really important post and news has a particularly special charm. Time to start catching up on your correspondence...

1. First, paint sequences of colours on the watercolour paper, then let them dry thoroughly. In the meantime, make a copy of the templates (p.166). Of course, you could also create and cut out your own shapes.

2. Now cut out the individual letters and shapes from your colourful watercolour paper and stick them onto the writing paper. Lay the individual sheets and envelopes between a couple of books overnight. This will press them nice and flat.

CAMERA STRAP

Sew a carry strap

Difficulty ★★☆
Time needed 1 hour
You will need
simple camera strap (usually supplied along
with your camera)
embroidery or nail scissors
robust fabric
sewing machine with heavy needle, & appropriate thread
iron

*Like many people, we love taking photographs. We always
have our camera with us! A pretty strap is essential for
keeping your camera conveniently to hand without looking
like a member of the paparazzi. The camera will hang
securely round your neck on the strap so you'll never
accidentally lose it, and the custom-made strap will
complement your unique style.*

1. First cut off both of the imitation leather ends with the
loops for attaching the camera strap. You can cut open
the fine stitching quite easily with a pair of nail scissors.

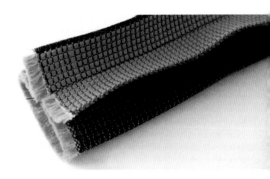

2. Cut out a long strip from your fabric: the size will
depend on the width of the end pieces and the length
of your strap, add an extra 4cm (1⅝in) to the width as
a seam allowance. Sew it into a tube, wrong side out.

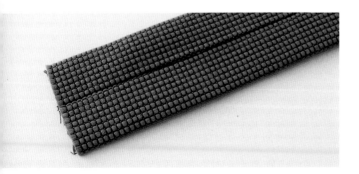

3. Now turn the tube right side out and iron it flat. Take
care when doing this that the seam runs central and not
to one side, so that when you're wearing the strap you
won't see the seam.

4. Finally, sew the strap back into the end attachment
pieces. A strong sewing machine needle should cope
with this, alternatively you could also sew it by hand.

Recycling boxes

Difficulty ★ ★ ★
Time needed 10 minutes per box + drying time
You will need
old cardboard boxes with slip-on lids (eg shoe boxes)
pretty wrapping paper
utility knife, ruler
spray adhesive

Old cardboard boxes and some pretty wrapping paper can be used to make wonderful boxes. Attractive boxes can also be used for organizational purposes - you can stash all kinds of stuff inside them - or even as gift boxes. We use them in our studio to house various materials and keep them tidily stacked in the cupboard. From something old, to something useful.

1. Depending on how big your box is, cut out a piece of wrapping paper large enough to completely cover it, with some to spare. Do the same for the lid, using a different paper, if you like.

2. Spray a little adhesive onto the middle of the back of the wrapping paper and place the open box on top. Cut in diagonally from all four corners of the wrapping paper towards the box corners.

3. Spray one of the narrow sides of the paper and tip the box onto the narrow side, so that the paper sticks to it. Now make two cuts in the overhanging paper and stick it around the box edge and into the inside.

4. Repeat this with the remaining three sides of the box until it is completely wrapped in the paper. Leave the spray adhesive to dry for a few minutes while you cover the lid of the box.

PRETTY STORAGE

ADVENT CALENDAR

45

Make a countdown calendar

Difficulty ★ ☆ ☆
Time needed 30 minutes
You will need
25 little envelopes of wood veneer paper, each 9.5 × 7 cm
(3¾ × 2¾in)
black foam board, 42 × 55 cm (16¾ × 22in)
all-purpose adhesive
wooden numbers from 1–24

How about a more grown-up version of an advent calendar? These mini wooden envelopes offer plenty of room for little thoughts and affectionate messages. To sweeten the pre-Christmas waiting period for your loved one in a truly stylish manner, all you have to do is think up 24 little heart-felt offerings.

Leaving an equal-sized border, stick all 25 envelopes onto the foam board with a blob of all-purpose adhesive. This works best if you lay out all the envelopes before you start, so that they don't end up being stuck to the board lopsided. Stick the numbers centrally on the lower part of the envelopes. In the 25th envelope you could package up something extra-special.

MAKE-UP BAG

Silk painting and bag sewing

Difficulty ★ ★ ☆
Time needed 2–3 hours + drying time
You will need
candle, dark blue silk dye, iron, & silver fabric pen
strong cotton fabric, approx 40 × 100 cm (16 × 40in)
scissors, pins, suitable thread, sewing machine, & button
grosgrain ribbon 8mm (³⁄₈in) wide
sheet of 3mm- (¹⁄₈in-) thick felt, 30 × 20 cm (12 × 8in)

This cool make-up bag is a favourite item and we really couldn't do without it any more. It comes along on every journey and other versions have also been proven to be a fabulous gift for friends! The water-inspired dye design is really individual and each bag is absolutely unique. Whether you use it for make-up or important documents, this bag is absolutely perfect!

1. To create the beautiful colour gradations on your fabric you will work with silk dye and wax. Light the candle and drip the wax onto the fabric in a random pattern. All the spots where wax is located will later be colourless. Now dampen the material slightly and drizzle little drops of silk dye over it.

2. Let the fabric dry out, then drip fresh wax onto it, repeating the entire process as many times as needed until you are satisfied with the result. Let the material dry, then iron off the wax using kitchen paper between the iron and the wax. Use the silver pen to make little sparkling highlights on the design. On the next pages we will show you how simple it is to sew your bag.

1. Cut out a piece from your fabric measuring 92 x 29cm (36¾ x 11⅝in). Make the incision marks where indicated on the template (p.167).

2. Fold the fabric in half with right sides facing outwards. Now fold back the fabric on each side until the incision marks are aligned with the central fold. On both sides you will see the reverse side of the material. Pin in place.

3. Sew up the open side edges. At the same time, hem the 1cm (⅜in) turnover (see template). Sew in a little loop of ribbon in the centre of one of the flaps.

4. This is how your sewn up bag should look, before you turn it right side out.

5. Cut out a rectangular piece of felt measuring 26.3 × 16 cm. (10⅜ × 6⅜ in).

6. Turn the bag right side out and put the felt sheet into the rear compartment, as shown here. This will make the back of the bag more stable.

7. Now you can sew up the final open seam along the already-stitched edge of the flap. Finally, sew on the button to align with the ribbon loop.

Super tip

It is always worth visiting a haberdashery store when trying to match buttons up with a piece of sewing you've worked hard on. Take your work to the store with you, so you can find the perfect button match.

PAPER BAG
LANTERNS

Silhouette paper cutting

Difficulty ★ ★ ★
Time needed 30 minutes
You will need paper bag lanterns made of flame-retardant paper, some pieces of thick card, utility knife, & tea lights

Shops stock a whole variety of designs of highly flame-retardant lantern bags. But, of course, it's even nicer to make your own! The bags must be lined with a special coating so they can't catch fire. Depending on the time of year, you can cut out holiday designs, or simple geometric patterns. As the days get shorter and tea lights flicker inside the lantern bags, your house will feel really cosy.

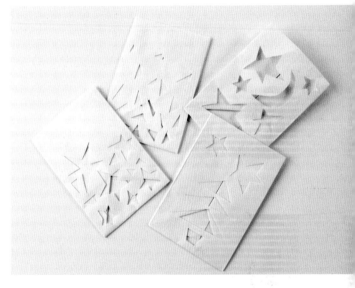

1. Lay thick card inside each lantern bag for protection, so that you don't damage the rear side of the bag when you are cutting out the shapes.

2. Cut out the design of your choice. Stars and triangles are really easy shapes to cut out of the paper. Take care that the uncut paper areas between the shapes are big enough, otherwise the paper may rip later. Place the tea lights inside your lanterns.

"One always has time enough, if one will apply it well."

Johann Wolfgang von Goethe

Make your own bird feeder

Difficulty ★ ★ ★
Time needed 2 hours
You will need coconut oil, bird food, twigs, clay pots, beeswax, & string

Anyone with a garden or balcony will be thrilled with this project. Instead of buying fat balls for the birds at your garden centre, you can make something much nicer yourself! This little bird meal is quick to make and your feathered friends will be so grateful. These days, you should feed the birds throughout the year. Thanks to man's impact on the environment, food supplies for wild birds are becoming ever more scarce and an increasing number of birds are dependent on our help, particularly during the breeding season.

Melt the coconut oil over a low heat and stir in the bird food until you have a thick consistency. Let the whole thing cool down slightly until the oil begins to solidify. In the meantime, stick twigs into the flower pots using a clump of beeswax. The hole should be sealed closed. Now pour the seedy-oil mixture into the pots and let it cool thoroughly. Hang the finished pots amongst the branches and shrubs using pieces of string.

Take care to hang the pots high enough, otherwise cats will find it all too easy to pounce on the birds you have enticed into your garden.

BIRD FEEDER POTS

CANDLE
WREATH

Working with wooden beads

Difficulty ★ ★ ☆
Time needed 1–2 hours
You will need
steel ring, 40cm (16in) in diameter
universal pliers
4 wooden beads, each 3cm (1¼in) in diameter
70 wooden beads, each 1.5cm (⅝in) in diameter
160 wooden beads, each 1cm (⅜in) in diameter

red gift ribbon, 1.5cm (⅝in) wide
glue gun
8 candle holders
8 candles
scissors
yarn needle
baker's twine

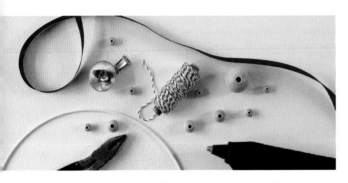

1. Cut through the steel ring in one place using the universal pliers, then thread on the beads and ribbon in the correct order (p.168).

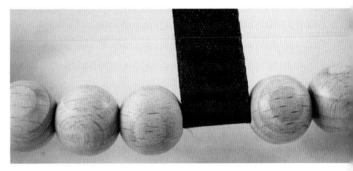

2. Stick one of the ribbon loops in place with a blob from the glue gun. Adjust the beads as needed. Attach the candle holders, similarly using the glue gun.

3. Depending on how wide the ribbon is and how big the candle holders are, you may need to occasionally discard a bead in order for everything to fit. Once you are done, reseal the ring by using a blob of hot glue inside a wooden bead to secure the two ends.

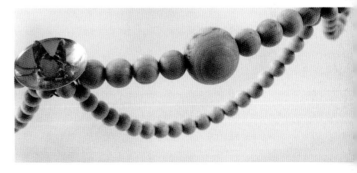

4. Finally, use the needle to thread 20 little wooden beads onto a 2m (6ft 8in) piece of baker's twine. Tie the start of the twine under a candle holder and loop in along to the next. Continue all around the ring and secure the end. Add the candles. Hang the wreath by its ribbons.

FESTIVE CROCKERY

50

Porcelain painting

Difficulty ★ ★ ★

Time needed 5 minutes per plate + drying time

You will need golden-edged china from a second-hand shop, gold porcelain paint, small shallow bowl, & various brushes

A festive table needs festive crockery. With porcelain paint and a bit of practice you can create your own totally unique tableware. Anyone who enjoys inviting friends and family over for meals will score a winner with this beautiful project.

Put the porcelain paint into a little bowl. Use the brushes to dab the paint onto the edges of the plates and bowls. Every brush will produce a unique shape. Let the paint dry, then bake the crockery in the oven following the paint manufacturer's instructions.

Make tree decorations

Difficulty ★ ★ ★

Time needed 1 hour

You will need strong card (400 g/m² [gsm]), utility knife, steel ruler, etching needle, & cotton thread

Even at the holidays not everyone wants to be kitsch - minimalist decorations and paper ornaments such as these are also very popular. This project is ideal for anyone who doesn't want their tree weighed down with expensive trinkets. These little pendants can be individually customized or just used as they are - roll on Christmas!

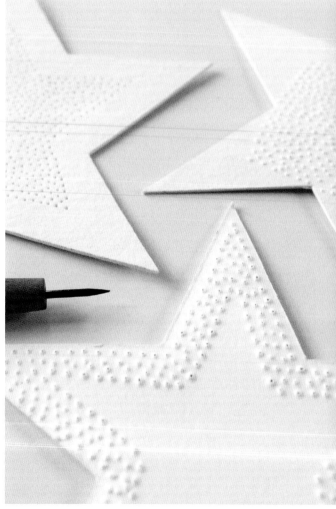

Cut out the stars using the templates (p.169). Use an etching needle to prick lots of little holes into the paper, in the pattern of your choice, protecting the work surface underneath with a piece of wood or similar. The result will be a delicate pattern through which light can shine. Hang up the stars using pieces of cotton thread.

PAPER STARS

PLACE CARDS

Table decorating

Difficulty ★ ☆ ☆
Time needed 30 minutes
You will need
dried flowers or seeds
old clothes pegs (one per person)
glue gun
instant camera with a mini format

Hosting lunch at your place? These homemade place cards will truly come into their own. We used an instant camera for this project, but it's also possible to use old pictures or printed photos. The pictures not only help your guests find their places, but also work well as an "ice breaker" if your diners don't all know each other already. Great fun!

Stick the dried flowers or seeds onto the old clothes pegs with a blob of glue. Put the pegs on the table at each place setting. In the middle of the peg there is space for a little photo of every diner. Here we used old childhood photographs of each guest, but it's more fun to get them to take instant photos of each other!

BASIC KNITTING COURSE

Everyone loves knitted items, though learning to knit can be an offputting hurdle for many people. But, rest assured, it is easier than you think to start knitting yourself, and you only need to know a few basics to quickly achieve wonderful results. Learning to knit really does take no time at all... and perfecting your knitting just takes practice. In the following step-by-steps we show the "Continental" style of knitting used by the authors, where you hold the working yarn in your left hand, but there are many different ways to knit.

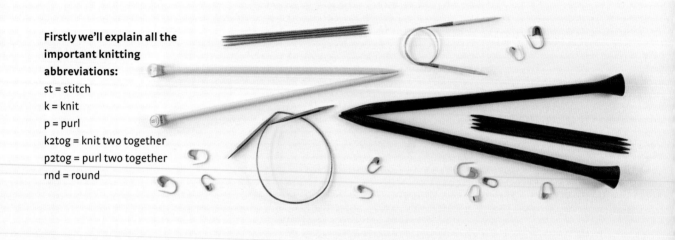

Firstly we'll explain all the important knitting abbreviations:

st = stitch

k = knit

p = purl

k2tog = knit two together

p2tog = purl two together

rnd = round

Make a slip knot

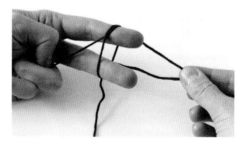

1. Wrap the wool around the index finger and middle finger of your left hand.

2. With your right hand, pull a loop of wool through both fingers on your left hand, through the wrapped wool.

3. Pull it tight. Slip the loop onto your knitting needles and you can start casting on stitches.

Casting on

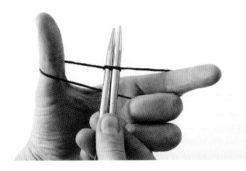

1. Hold the wool in your left hand as shown. The strand which runs over your index finger leads to the ball of wool.

2. Take both needles under the left strand coming from your thumb, then to the right under the strand from your index finger.

3. Take the needles to the left again and through the thumb loop from above.

4. Let the loop slip off your thumb and pull it tight on the needles. You will now have your second stitch on the needles. Continue until you have cast on the correct number of stitches.

Holding yarn and needles correctly

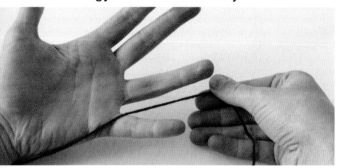

1. Take the wool between your ring finger and your little finger on your left hand.

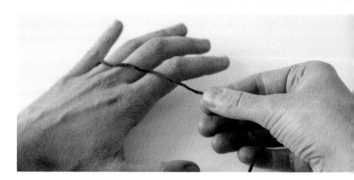

2. Take the wool over the back of your hand, then wrap it around your index finger twice.

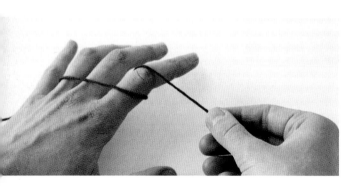

3. With your left index finger you can adjust the tension of the working wool.

4. As you work, hold the needle with the cast on stitches in your left hand. The right hand holds the needle that you knit with.

Knit stitches

1. To produce a knit stitch, lay the working wool, coming from your left index finger, behind the left needle. Poke the right needle into the first stitch on the left needle, going in through the front of the stitch.

2. Using the right needle, pick up the working wool from behind and pull it back through the stitch to the front.

3. Now let the old stitch slip off of the left needle and the new stitch onto the right needle.

4. Your first knit stitch is now on the right needle. Repeat as many times as instructed, keeping the tension even.

Purl stitches

1. To produce a purl stitch, lay the working wool in front of the left needle. Poke the right needle into the first stitch on the left needle from behind.

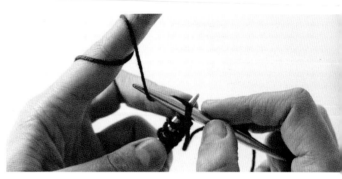

2. Pick up the working wool by wrapping the strand once around your right needle, then pull it back through the stitch.

3. Now let the old stitch slip off of the left needle and the new stitch onto the right needle.

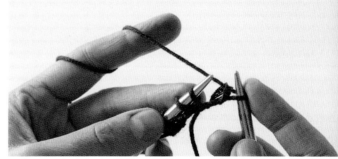

4. Your first purl stitch is now on the right needle. Repeat as many times as instructed, keeping the tension even.

Decreasing knitwise and purlwise

knitwise

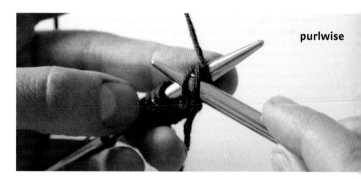

purlwise

For a simple knit decrease, knit two stitches together. Work as for a normal knit stitch, but instead of inserting your right needle through the front of one stitch, insert it through two stitches. When you've completed the decrease only one stitch will remain on the right needle.

For a simple purl decrease, purl two stitches together. Work as for a normal purl stitch, but instead of inserting your right needle through the back of one stitch, insert it through two stitches. When you've completed the decrease only one stitch will remain on the right needle.

Knitting in the round

1. The cast on stitches should loosely cover the circular needle. All stitches point inwards. Place a stitch marker on the needle if you wish.

2. Hold the needle with the working wool in your right hand and the needle with the first stitch in your left hand.

3. Now knit the stitches from the left onto the right needle. This is how you join in the round. Every time you pass the stitch marker it is one round (or row).

145

BASIC CROCHET COURSE

Crocheting is such fun and, with these basics, you'll soon know the most important tricks of the trade. Over the next four pages we will briefly explain the most important terms and techniques. Grab your hook, get set, go!

Hold hook and yarn correctly

1. To cast on the first stitches, tie a little loop near the start of the wool (see "making a slip knot" on page 140 in the basic knitting course).

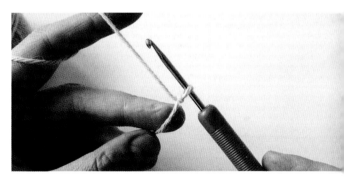

2. Hold the wool in your left hand – exactly as you do for knitting. The crochet hook is held in your right hand.

Crocheting chain stitches

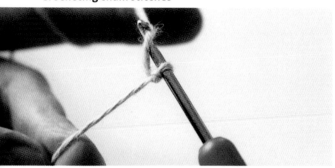 

1. To make a chain stitch, insert the crochet hook through the slipknot and pull the working wool back through with the help of the hook.

2. Cast on as many chain stitches with your hook as specified in the pattern instructions. The stitches will form a chain.

Double crochet stitches

1. To make your first double crochet stitch, insert the hook into the second chain stitch (counting from the needle outwards) and pull the working wool back through this stitch. There are now two stitches on the hook.

2. Now fetch the wool once more through both of these stitches. Repeat both of these steps until you reach the end of your row. Before every new row always crochet an extra chain stitch to bring the stitches up to the correct height for the next row.

Crocheting a sphere

1. Cast on six chain stitches and join them in the round by working a double crochet stitch into the first chain stitch. The subsequent stitches will be crocheted in the round.

2. Crochet the following rounds as per the relevant instructions and gradually a hemisphere shape will form.

Increasing stitches

1. You increase stitches by crocheting twice into the same stitch. Work one double crochet stitch into the first stitch in the usual way.

2. Then, insert the hook into the first double crochet stitch again and work a second double crochet in the same stitch.

Decreasing stitches

1. To decrease stitches, insert the hook through the first stitch and pull the yarn through once. Now there are two stitches on your hook.

2. Keeping the two stitches on your hook, insert the hook through the next stitch and pull the yarn through. Now there are three stitches on your hook.

3. Finally, pull the yarn through all three stitches. You have now decreased one stitch.

4. By decreasing stitches, the diameter of each round reduces and the sphere gradually closes.

BASIC EMBROIDERY & SEWING COURSE

Knowing basic embroidery and sewing stitches can come in very handy in life. Anyone who can quickly sew on a button, darn a hole, or repair a small seam knows how practical these skills are. Over the next pages we will show you the basic stitches for successfully tackling embroidery and sewing projects by hand.

Running stitch

Weave the needle through the fabric in and out along the stitching line. The spacing on the rear side determines the stitch length on the upper side.

Back stitch

Back stitch creates a continuous line of stitches without gaps and uses twice as much thread on the back side as on the front side.

Blanket stitch

Secure the thread to the fabric with a little knot. Then stitch through in one spot and pull the thread through completely. Poke the needle through the fabric again nearby, wrap the thread around the needle and pull the thread tight.

Satin stitch

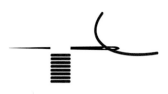

Using satin stitch you can cover surfaces or embroider graphic patterns. You can vary the length and angle of your stitches. However, individual stitches shouldn't be too long or they will catch and distort.

Cross stitch

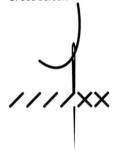

First embroider the diagonal lines from left to right, then turn these into crosses by working back across the row. Cross stitch works particularly well on woven fabric.

Upright cross stitch

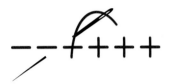

An upright cross stitch is worked exactly like a normal cross stitch, except that the crosses are rotated by 45 degrees.

Half stitch

The half stitch is often used in Gobelin tapestry work and so is also referred to as Gobelin stitch. Work stitches in a row at the same angle and height.

Bookbinding stitch – Japanese style

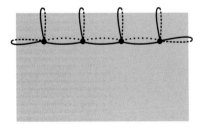

Using this bookbinding technique, you can stitch together pages for both thin volumes and larger books with a simple sewn binding (p.32).

EMBROIDERY LETTERS FOR NOTEBOOKS

Project (p.20): Scale the embroidery pattern to your desired size using a photocopier. For an A6-sized booklet, scale up the letters by approximately 180%. For an A5 book, scale up the letters by approximately 250%.

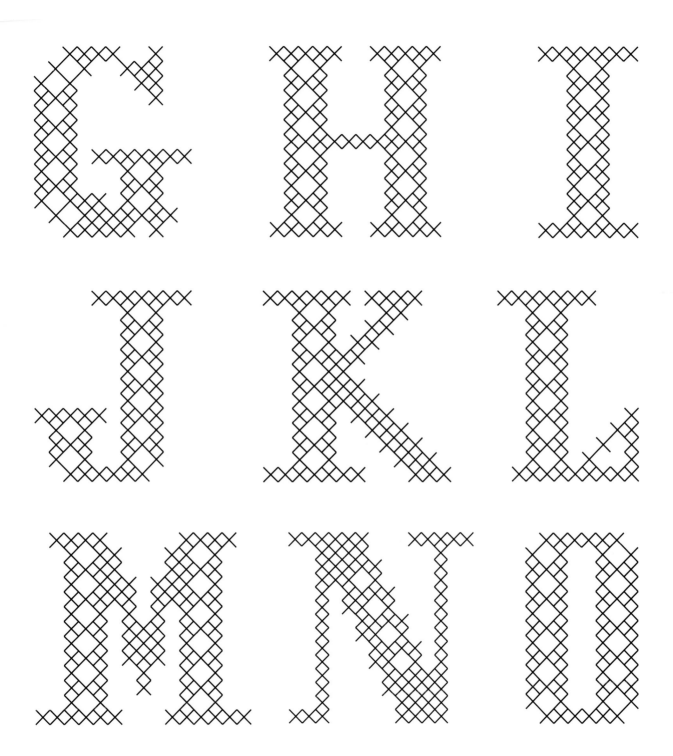

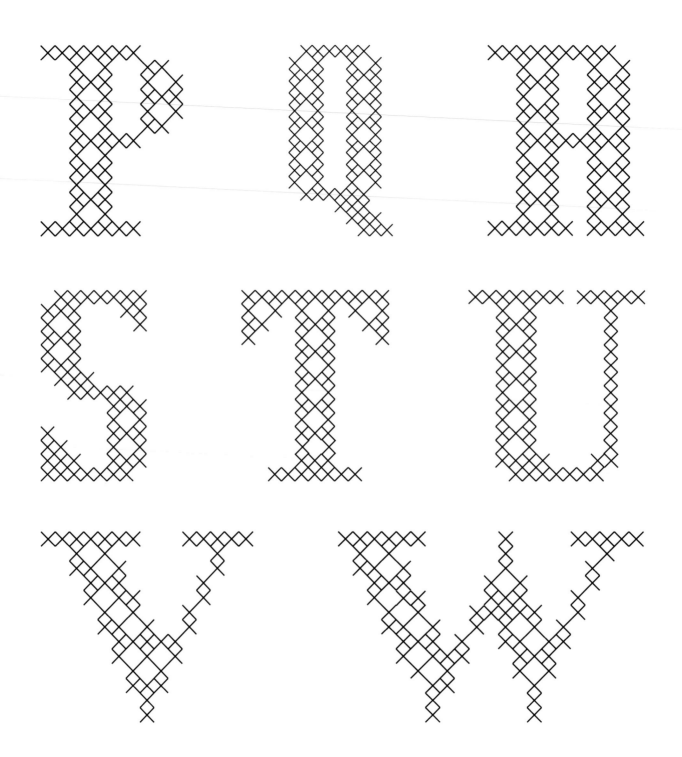

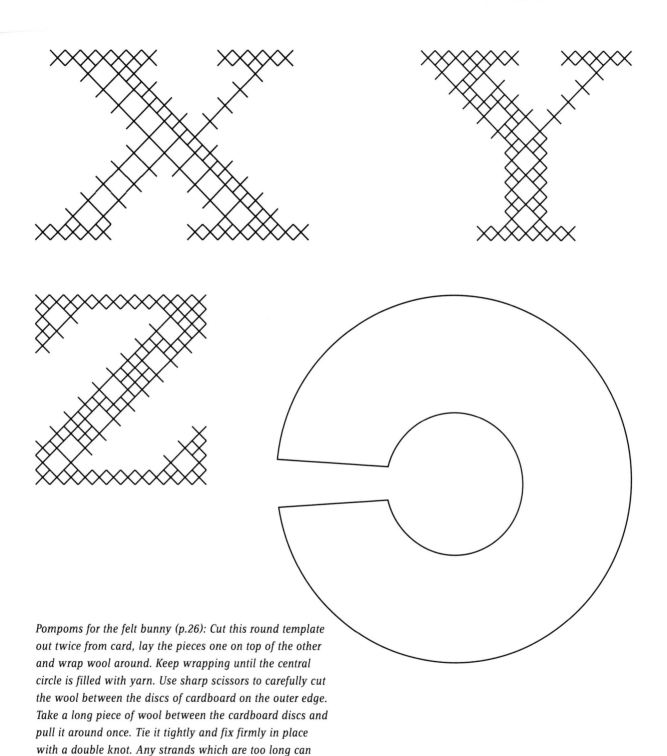

Pompoms for the felt bunny (p.26): Cut this round template out twice from card, lay the pieces one on top of the other and wrap wool around. Keep wrapping until the central circle is filled with yarn. Use sharp scissors to carefully cut the wool between the discs of cardboard on the outer edge. Take a long piece of wool between the cardboard discs and pull it around once. Tie it tightly and fix firmly in place with a double knot. Any strands which are too long can be trimmed to length with scissors.

TRAVEL WALLET PATTERN TEMPLATE

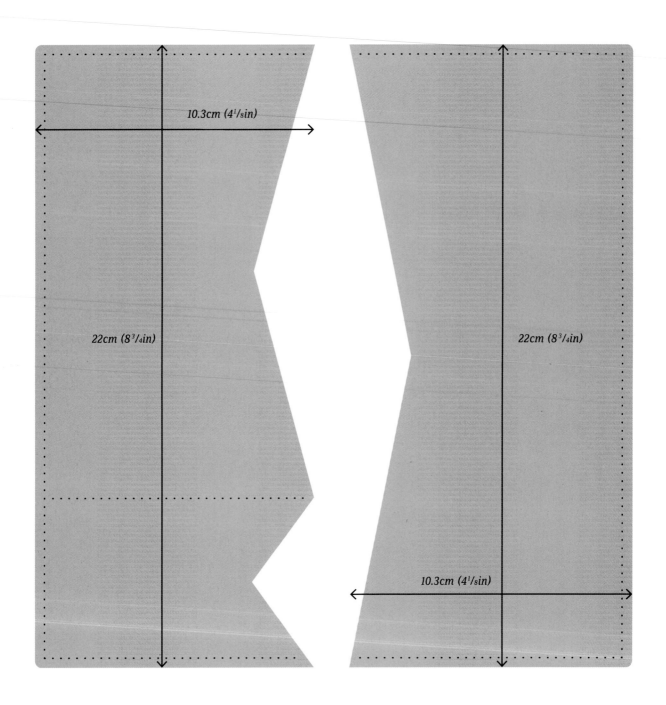

10.3cm (4^1/$_8$in)

22cm (8^3/$_4$in)

22cm (8^3/$_4$in)

10.3cm (4^1/$_8$in)

Project (p.22): these three sections cut from leather (or felt) are what you need for the travel wallet. Scale up the sections by 125% using a photocopier. We have illustrated the final desired size by annotating each template accordingly. You can round off the corners using sharp scissors.

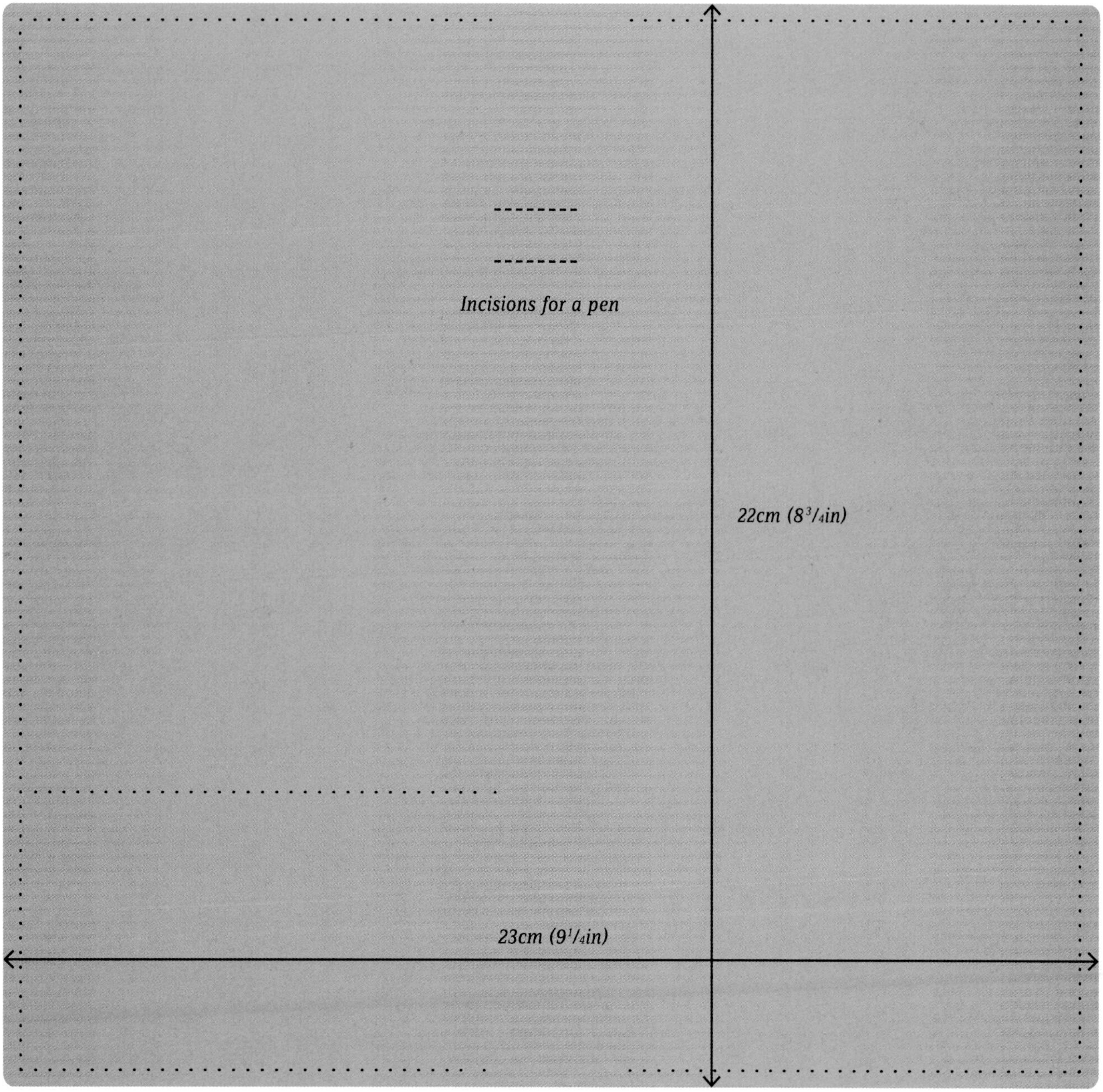

- - - - - - - -

- - - - - - - -

Incisions for a pen

22cm (8³/₄in)

23cm (9¹/₄in)

FELT BUNNY PATTERN TEMPLATE

Project (p.26): Scale up the template for the bunny by 125% using a photocopier. The light grey ears illustrate where and at what angle they should eventually be sewn in. You need to cut out two templates for each body and ear.

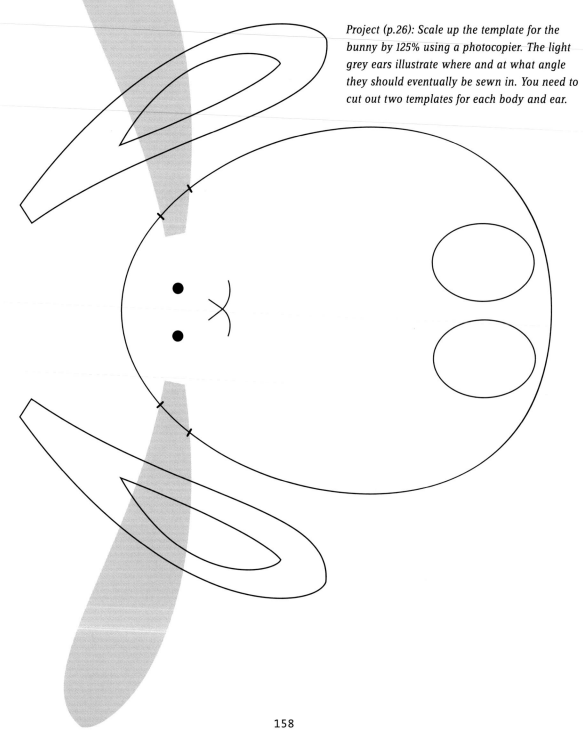

RUCKSACK PATTERN TEMPLATE

Project (p.40): Transfer the pattern template for the rucksack in its actual size onto brown paper or newspaper. We have annotated it with the actual dimensions, the seam allowance is already included in the calculations. Cut out the fabric to be twice as big by placing the dashed line on the edge of the folded fabric.

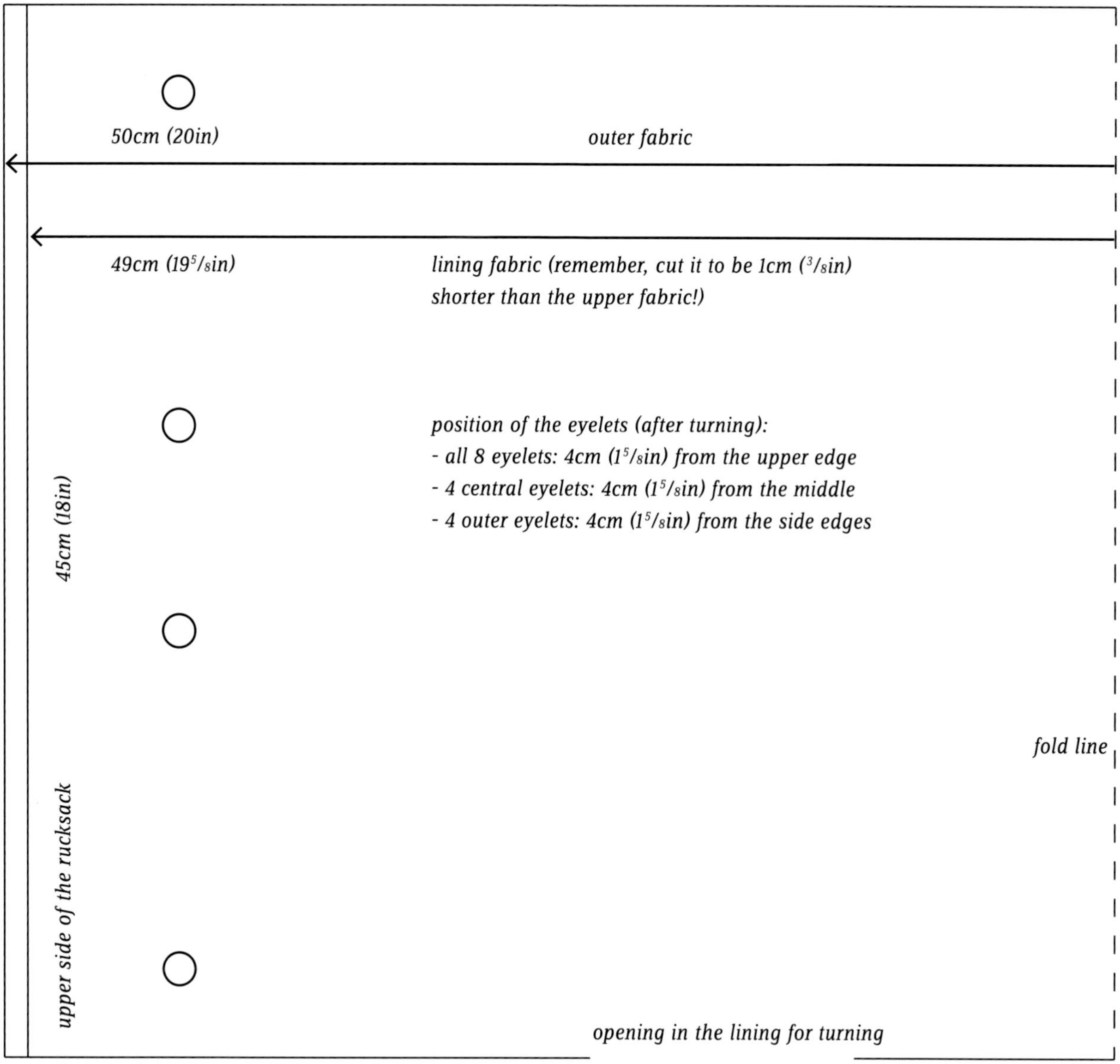

50cm (20in)   outer fabric

49cm (19⁵/₈in)   *lining fabric (remember, cut it to be 1cm (³/₈in) shorter than the upper fabric!)*

position of the eyelets (after turning):
- *all 8 eyelets: 4cm (1⁵/₈in) from the upper edge*
- *4 central eyelets: 4cm (1⁵/₈in) from the middle*
- *4 outer eyelets: 4cm (1⁵/₈in) from the side edges*

45cm (18in)

fold line

upper side of the rucksack

opening in the lining for turning

ESPADRILLES PATTERN TEMPLATE

Project (p.58): The pattern template for the espadrilles was provided to us by kind permission of the Prym company and is subject to their copyright. When purchasing the Prym shoe soles you will also find the pattern template in its actual size. The template in this book must first be enlarged by 150%. It contains no seam allowances! For the toe (top diagram) you will need two pieces each (one reversed) of upper fabric and lining fabric. For the heel (lower diagram) you will also need two pieces each of upper and lining fabric.

The relevant sizes are determined by the different dotted lines. From the outside in:

1. Shoe size UK9 (EU42)
2. Shoe size UK8 (EU41)
3. Shoe size UK6–7 (EU39–40)
4. Shoe size UK5 (EU38)
5. Shoe size UK3–4 (EU36–37)

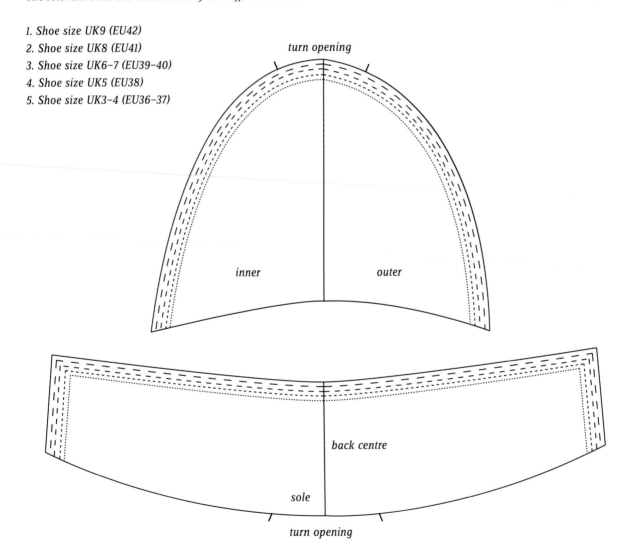

turn opening

inner   outer

back centre

sole

turn opening

BAG TYPESCRIPT

Project (p.64): Scale up the lettering for the gym bag by 125%. It will work even better if you create the lettering yourself on a computer and print it onto the film, that way you can choose the font you like best. Make sure you have the copyright permission for your selected font, if choosing a different one.

WALL ORGANIZER PATTERN TEMPLATE

Project (p.82): We have sketched the individual felt cut-outs for you here, annotated with the relevant actual dimensions. Of course you are free to cut your own sized version to suit your individual needs.

1 *45×34cm (18×13⁵/₈in)*
2 *20×30cm (8×12in), laid out in two folds divided by a seam – to stick newspapers in*
3 *20×6.5cm (8×2⁵/₈in)*
4 *26×13cm (10³/₈in×5¹/₄in)*
5 *30×11.5cm (12×4⁵/₈in), gently slanted and with various vertical seams to accommodate pens, brushes and so on*
6 *9.5×15cm (3³/₄×6in)*

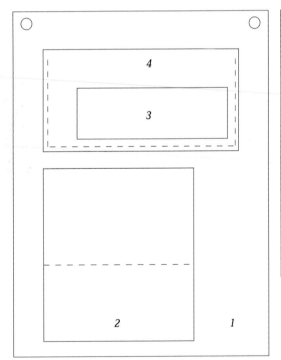

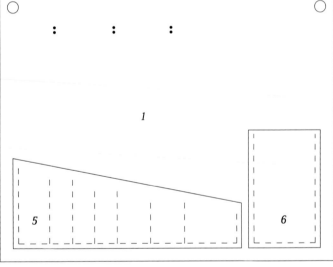

FABRIC SMOCKING TECHNIQUES

Project (p.86): Here we will show you three quite simple techniques for smocking material. The thinner the fabric, the smaller the pattern on the fabric can be.

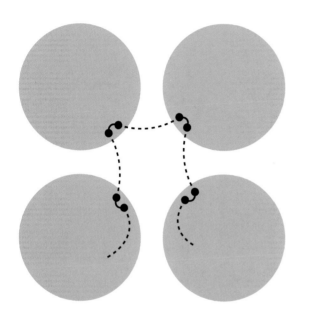

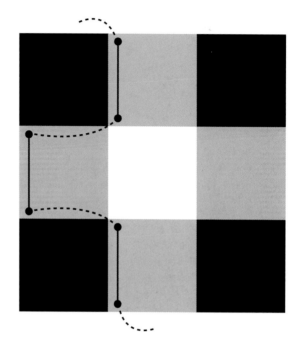

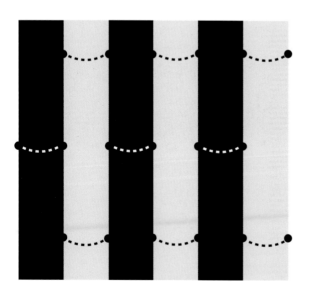

1. Polka dot pattern: Work in groups of four dots. Stitch up from behind one of the dots, then back through to the rear of the fabric right next to the first stitch. Next, bring the needle back up in the next adjacent dot, then back down, and so on. Gather the four dots together by pulling on the thread. Move on to the next four dots.

2. Checked pattern: Stitch in alternate squares (here grey) from two columns. Pull the thread together always on the same side of the squares (here, the left). This produces a series of triangles.

3. Striped pattern: Stitch in two opposite points, pull them together and tie both the thread ends together on the rear of the fabric. Alternate from row to row to form diamonds.

PURSE PATTERN TEMPLATE

Project (p.106): Embroider the pattern for the little purse in half cross stitch (p.151) on the cross stitch fabric. You can select the individual colours to suit your own taste. The basic pattern with the different colours is shown here.

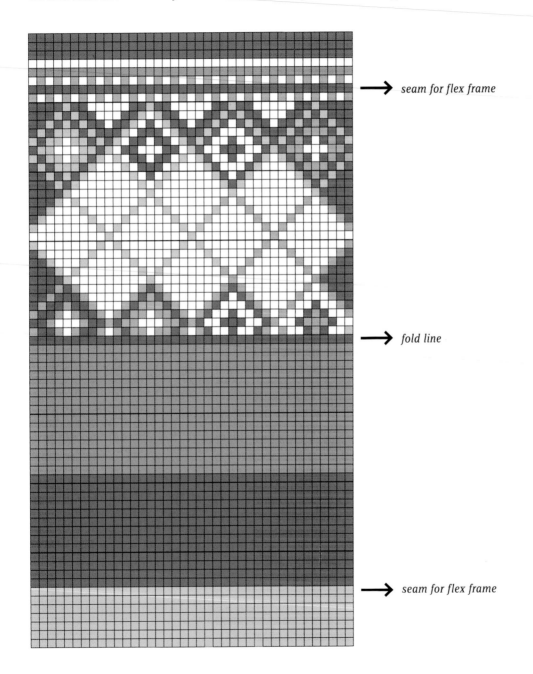

→ seam for flex frame

→ fold line

→ seam for flex frame

FELT BAG PATTERN TEMPLATE

Project (p.114): Scale up the pattern template for the felt bag to the size you need. The black dots are stamped out using a hollow punch. The grey lines are stitched with wool.

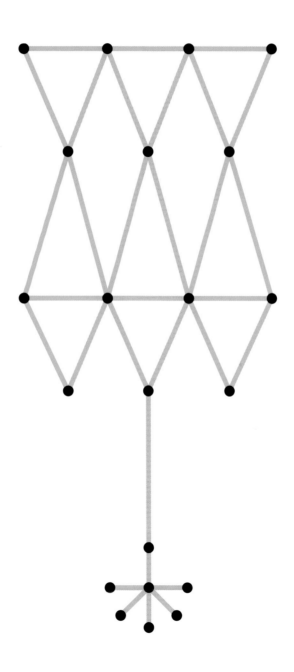

STATIONERY TEMPLATES

Project (p.116): Copy the letters and shapes onto an extra sheet of paper and transfer these back to front (as if in a mirror) onto the rear side of your dried watercolour sheet.

MAKE-UP BAG PATTERN TEMPLATE

Project (p.124): For best results, you should transfer the pattern template for the make-up bag onto brown paper or newspaper. Make sure to mark in all the incision locations. The seam allowance is already included. The 1cm ($^3/_8$in) on both edges will be hemmed.

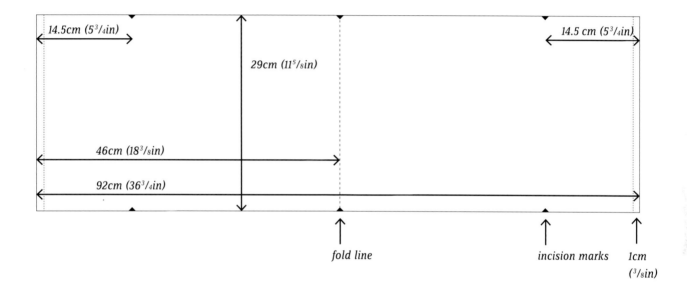

14.5cm ($5^3/_4$in)

29cm ($11^5/_8$in)

46cm ($18^3/_8$in)

92cm ($36^3/_4$in)

14.5 cm ($5^3/_4$in)

fold line

incision marks

1cm ($^3/_8$in)

CANDLE WREATH TEMPLATE

Project (p.132): Here we show you the sequence for the various elements in the candle wreath. Depending on how wide your ribbon is and how big the candle holders are, the quantity of little wooden beads 1.5cm (⁵/₈in) in diameter can be adjusted to fit.

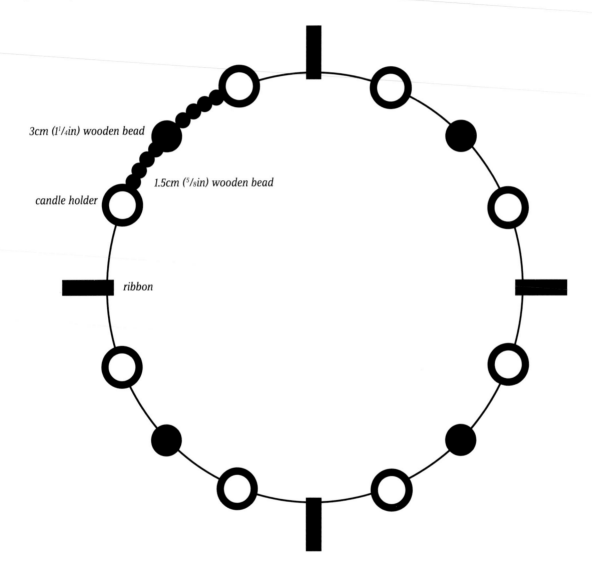

3cm (1¹/₄in) wooden bead

1.5cm (⁵/₈in) wooden bead

candle holder

ribbon

PAPER STARS TEMPLATE

Project (p.136): Copy the stars onto an extra sheet of paper and transfer the outlines onto the rear side of your card.

MANUFACTURERS & SUPPLIERS

Using high-quality tools and materials is important for the success of your projects. All craftspeople know that good tools are essential. Make sure you focus on quality to avoid your hobby becoming frustrating and to make sure you have fun whilst working.

Here in Berlin we love to get inspiration from the range at the Modulor shop. The choice of materials and artistic supplies at this specialist shop is really impressive. Artists and architects will find everything they need for their work, and crafters and DIY enthusiasts who find themselves in the city will discover it's really worth a visit! www.modulor.de

For our UK-based readers, materials and tools can be bought from these online manufacturers and suppliers:

artistic supplies: Great Art – www.greatart.co.uk
baker's twines: James Lever – www.jameslever.co.uk
ceramic transfer film: Crafty Computer Paper – www.craftycomputerpaper.co.uk
dyes: The Dye Shop – www.thedyeshop.co.uk
espadrille soles: Prym – www.prym-consumer.com
fabric: Croft Mill – www.croftmill.co.uk
haberdashery and interior decor: John Lewis – www.johnlewis.co.uk
handicraft materials: Homecrafts – www.homecrafts.co.uk
jewellery-making accessories: Creative Beadcraft – www.creativebeadcraft.co.uk
leather and accessories: Artisan Leather – www.artisanleather.co.uk
Lumi Inkodye: Lumi Inkodye – www.inkodye.com/international
office supplies: Avery – www.avery.co.uk
textiles, yarns, and accessories: Hoooked – www.hoooked.co.uk
wool and needles: Ball and Needle – www.ballandneedle.co.uk

And, of course, we ourselves offer a whole range of kits and other materials.
We look forward to you visiting our website: www.supercraftlab.com

ABOUT THE AUTHORS

We are Catharina Bruns and Sophie Pester. We are both designers and founders of Supercraft; creative DIY kits and shop for special materials for anyone who enjoys making lovely things themselves.

We love making things. We love our work. And because we love what we do so much, we have instigated not just one, but numerous projects together. Alongside our work on Supercraft we organise the annual "hello handmade" market in Hamburg. "Hello handmade" is a design market for handmade products and original concepts. On the one hand we run it to provide an outlet for creative freelancers and, on the other hand, to bring the amazing work and craftspeople to the attention of as many people as possible. We invite around 80 designers and small labels to sell their products and are delighted to host more than 5,000 visitors per day. Will you come next time too? We'd love that!
www.hello-handmade.com

We know how vital it is to write down your ideas and, most importantly, to implement them, so we founded "Lemon Books" a design platform and manufacturer of personalised notebooks. You can create your own notebooks quickly and easily, straight from your computer, or you can select some from our collection.
www.lemonbooks.de (note: this is a German language website)

An independent culture of doing it yourself is also the topic of Catharina's first book "work is not a job - you decide what work is!", published by Campus Verlag. The project of the same name "workisnotajob" also concerns itself with self-sufficiency and a new kind of working culture which embraces independence and self-realisation. The book is a passionate plea for a new attitude to work - an entrepreneurial approach which we realise in our projects every day. An inspiration for anyone else who sees their work as more than just a "job".
www.workisnotajob.com/en

And because we are so interested in different working options, we regularly interview other people who shape their own working environments and forge new models of working through their projects. With "superwork" we want to inspire and help people to think and work differently.
www.super-work.com (note: this is a German language website)

All of our projects have one thing in common: we want to inspire people to discover their own creative powers. We believe that the most important experiences and the finest things in life have to be created by you. And then spread the word that it can be done. Do it yourself!

www.supercraftlab.com

ACKNOWLEDGEMENTS

Many thanks for reading and crafting with us! We really hope that you have got stuck in to lots of projects and have been stimulated to create your own ideas.

Working on this kind of book is lots of fun and involves many helping hands. We would particularly like to thank our families, our parents, and grannies who always believe in us and have helped out themselves – with huge affection – on one or another project.

We are also particularly indebted to our photographer Anne Deppe. She has taken fabulous pictures for this book and captured the spirit of Supercraft perfectly. We had so much fun at every photo shoot (as you can see from the Polaroid pictures on the left! Anne is on the far right in the central picture). It's really worth visiting Anne's website: www.annedeppe.de

Of course we would also like to thank DK publishers who found us and who we have loved working with to produce this book. A particular thank you to Monika Schlitzer, Katharina May, and Sophie Schiela for their wonderful collaboration!

Thanks also go to all our friends, acquaintances, and DIY heroes, to our favourite stores, and to the fabulous producers who we have so enjoyed working with:

Ursula Heinrich
Lisa Kächeler from Modulor
Birgit Hahn from Garn & Mehr (Yarn & More)
Jana Eichwald and Carmen Follmann-Krämer from Prym GmbH
Steffi Wilke from Das Lederparadies (Leather Paradise)
Ilona Brinkmann from Hoooked
Nina Zweiffel from Zweiffel Einrichtung
Nancy and Moritz for dog sitting
Sabrina, André and Jule; Tim; Piet; Bo; and Camillo for letting us use their fabulous homes.

British edition

Translator Alison Tunley

Editor Lucy Bannell

Project editor Kathryn Meeker

Senior art editor Glenda Fisher

Jacket designer Amy Keast

Senior pre-production producer Tony Phipps

Senior producer Stephanie McConnell

Creative technical support Sonia Charbonnier

Managing editor Stephanie Farrow

Managing art editor Christine Keilty

German edition

Photography Anne Deppe

Tutorial pictures Sophie Pester, Catharina Bruns

Illustrations and templates Sophie Pester, Catharina Bruns

Editing Anja Fuhrmann

Design Sophie Pester, Catharina Bruns

Production Sophie Schiela

Production coordination Katharina Dürmeier

Production management Dorothee Whittaker

Project support Katharina May

Editorial management Caren Hummel

Programme management Monika Schlitzer

First British Edition, 2016
Published in Great Britain by Dorling Kindersley Limited
80 Strand, London WC2R 0RL

Copyright © 2016 Dorling Kindersley Limited
A Penguin Random House Company

15 16 17 18   10 9 8 7 6 5 4 3 2 1
001 - 289747 - March/2016

A CIP catalogue record for this book is available from the British Library.

ISBN 978-0-2412-4227-8

Printed and bound in China

All images © Dorling Kindersley Limited
For further information see: www.dkimages.com

A WORLD OF IDEAS:
SEE ALL THERE IS TO KNOW
www.dk.com